Jobseeker's Guide

Fifth Edition

Training Handout for Ten Steps to a Federal Job® Workshops

By Kathryn Troutman, President of The Resume Place
with Paulina Chen, Designer

D1383335

The
Resume Place

89 Mellor Avenue
Baltimore, MD 21228
www.resume-place.com

331.11
T758

The Resume Place, Inc.
Federal Career Publishers

89 Mellor Avenue, Baltimore, MD 21228
Phone: 888-480-8265
www.resume-place.com
Email: resume@resume-place.com

Printed in the United States of America

Jobseeker's Guide, 5th Ed.
ISBN: 978-0-9824190-8-3

We have been careful to provide accurate federal job search information in this book, but it is possible that errors and omissions may have been introduced.

Attention Transition Counselors, Veterans' Representatives, Workforce Counselors, Career Counselors: The *Jobseeker's Guide* is a training program "handout" to support the Ten Steps to a Federal Job® workshops and PowerPoint program, which is taught at military bases, universities, one-stops, and DoD agencies worldwide. To be licensed to teach the Ten Steps to a Federal Job® curriculum as a Certified Federal Job Search Trainer™ or Certified Federal Career Coach® programs, go to www.resume-place.com for information on our train the trainer program. Since the program was developed in 2002, more than 1,000 have been licensed to teach Ten Steps to a Federal Job® with this guide as the handout.

AUTHOR'S NOTES: Sample resumes are real but fictionalized. All federal applicants have given permission for their resumes to be used as samples for this publication. Privacy policy is strictly enforced.

PUBLICATION TEAM:
Cover and Interior Page Design: Paulina Chen
Editors: Paulina Chen, Sandra Lee Keppley, Emily Troutman
Federal Resume Samples: Kathryn Troutman, Dottie Hendricks, Lex Levin
Contributor: Kimberly Hessler (LinkedIn Networking)
KSA / Questionnaire Chapter: Diane Hudson-Burns
Copyeditor: Pamela Sikora
Indexer: Christine Frank

"Over the past decade, nearly 3 million service members have transitioned back to civilian life, and more are joining them every day.

"When these men and women come home, they bring unparalleled skills and experience. ... They've saved lives in some of the toughest conditions imaginable. They've managed convoys and moved tons of equipment over dangerous terrain. They've tracked millions of dollars of military assets. They've handled pieces of equipment that are worth tens of millions of dollars. They do incredible work. Nobody is more skilled, more precise, more diligent, more disciplined.

"... These are the Americans we want to keep serving here at home as we rebuild this country. So we're going to do everything we can to make sure that when our troops come home, they come home to new jobs and new opportunities and new ways to serve their country."

– President Obama, February 3, 2012
Remarks at Fire Station 5, Arlington, Virginia

Dear Federal Jobseekers, Career Trainers, and Advisors,

For the first time in nine years, there are no American soldiers fighting in Iraq. The U.S. mission in Afghanistan is also changing. Our U.S. armed forces are facing a drawdown across all branches.

At the same time, the number of jobless veterans continues to outpace that of civilians. Federal jobs remain one of the most important resources available to separating and retiring personnel, but the system for applying is incredibly complex.

This fifth edition of the *Jobseeker's Guide* focuses on making the federal job process even simpler for applicants. I've included:

- Two new sample federal resumes—one for a military spouse and one for military personnel
- A new LinkedIn resume sample and new job fair resumes
- Navigation advice for the newest USAJOBS and ApplicationManager.gov application processes
- Category rating insight for understanding the hiring process
- More keyword lists, targeting the most popular series for military and spouses
- Latest information for spouse and veterans' preference programs, including Schedule A and PPP for Spouses

Army, Marine Corps, Navy, Air Force, Coast Guard, National Guard, and Air National Guard career counselors are teaching the Ten Steps to a Federal Job® workshop at military bases worldwide. I hope to see you soon in one of our classes.

Good luck with your federal job search,

Kathryn Troutman,
Author and Publisher

How Many Hats Do You Wear at Work?

Everyone wears different "hats" at work. The hats you wear at work are KEYWORDS for your federal resume. Make a list of 5 to 7 hats you wear everyday in your job. This exercise will help you write your federal resume with keywords (nouns and verbs) in the Outline Format. See more information in Step 5 on keywords and in Step 6 on federal resume writing in the Outline Format.

Examples of hats:

- *Supply Analyst*
- *Logistics Manager*
- *Transportation Specialist*
- *Supervisor*
- *Instructor*
- *Team Leader*
- *Database Administrator*
- *Research / Analyst*
- *Contract Officer*
- *Purchasing Specialist*
- *Office Administrator*
- *Timekeeper*

Your list of 5-7 hats:

_____

_____

_____

_____

_____

_____

_____

This is a federal job search campaign—not just a resume and application for a job. The most determined and persevering veterans and spouses WILL get hired into a stable career civilian position in government following all of these ten steps.

1. **Review the federal job process.** Start your federal job search with critical federal job information. Find out which agencies, job titles, and grade levels are best suited for you.

2. **Network.** Even with government, who you know is important. This information will remind you that your family, friends, and acquaintances may be a lead to a job in government. Learn strategies to introduce yourself and your job goals.

3. **Research vacancy announcements on USAJOBS.** Learn the fastest way to search for federal jobs on USAJOBS. Search for geographic location and salary first, then drill down to the jobs that sound right for you. You can't write a good federal resume without a target vacancy announcement—even if the announcement is a sample to get you started.

4. **Analyze your core competencies.** In addition to technical keywords and qualifications, your basic core competencies can help you stand out. Are you flexible, customer-focused, and creative? Do you demonstrate excellent team membership abilities, and work well under deadlines? Technical, specialized skills + great interpersonal skills = Best Qualified!

5. **Analyze vacancy announcements for keywords.** Learn how to find keywords in each announcement for your federal resume. Look for the keywords in Duties, Qualifications, Specialized Experience, and KSA lists. Add the keywords into your resume to make it readable, focused, and impressive.

6. **Write your Outline Format and paper federal resumes.** Feature your top skills and accomplishments for each position with keywords. Master the two formats: the Outline Format for online builders, and the paper format for interviews, email attachments, and browser uploads.

7. **KSAs in your federal resume and assessment questionnaires.** The "rated and ranked" KSAs have been eliminated, but various "how to apply" instructions may still list KSAs that should be covered in the resume. You will also find Assessment Questionnaires with Yes/No and multiple-choice questions.

8. **Apply for jobs with automated recruitment systems.** Carefully read the "how to apply" instructions, which could be different for each announcement. Get ready to copy and paste your resume into builders, answer questions, write short essays, and fax or upload your documents.

9. **Track and follow up your applications.** Don't just send in your application and forget about it; you have to manage your federal job search campaign. Learn how to call the personnel office to find out critical information for improving your future applications. Find out how to get your application score.

10. **Interview for a federal job.** Get tips to improve your chances with different types of interviews. Tell your best stories about your accomplishments and leadership skills. Be personable, passionate about the job, and sharp with our list of techniques.

Take a few minutes to write your information and accomplishments.

Please answer these questions:

What is your current or last job title?

What would you like to learn in this workshop?

Accomplishment Freewriting:

Describe an accomplishment from your current position or recent volunteer work. Accomplishments are critical for your federal resume, assessment questionnaire essays / examples, and behavior-based interviews.

Write at least three sentences here about your accomplishment:

_____

_____

_____

_____

_____

_____

_____

The bold type indicates the type of accomplishment these applicants have achieved—the skills and competencies they have demonstrated through their outstanding service.

TECHNICAL TEAMWORK IN EMERGENCY SITUATION

PLAYED A KEY ROLE IN SHIP'S DISASTER RECOVERY TEAM. Trained to switch to redundant backup systems without loss of command and control in the event of catastrophic equipment failure. Supervised five more junior communications staff. Participated in maritime protection / force interdiction operations in Iraqi territorial waters (North Persian Gulf) claimed by Iran and designed to protected Iraqi oil platforms from Iranian military incursions, February-March 2008.

SPECIAL ESSENTIAL RELIEF DEPLOYMENT FOR TSUNAMI RELIEF

CHOSEN FOR TSUNAMI RELIEF TEAM, 12/2004: Chosen for stand-by team after Indian Ocean Tsunami, and rapidly deployed to Southeast Asia for tsunami relief. Conducted essential relief operations for 3 months in tsunami-affected areas in Thailand, Sri Lanka, and the Maldives under harsh conditions.

MARKETING PROGRAM FOR MILITARY FAMILIES WITH FAMILY MEMBER IN IRAQ

Conceptualized a successful program for family members to send gifts and messages to military personnel. More than 2,500 messages were sent through this program in just six months. Sold business in less than six months for a substantial profit.

CREATIVE PRODUCTION AND MARKETING

Established a successful in-home business with local producers of business cards. Contracted with more than 15 vendors and tracked orders for more than 200 customers in two years. Efficiently set up and managed own schedule and schedule for automatic reordering.

OPERATIONS EFFICIENCY AND MISSION SUCCESS

In 2007, as an Operations Officer with the 77th Personnel Services Battalion, Armed Forces Overseas Germany, I developed a management system that increased efficiency of processing $90,000 in business travel vouchers and achieved 100 percent accuracy during the annual 2002 audit.

During this time, I single-handedly coordinated all Force Protection missions for all subordinate companies in five different communities. This involved expert planning and executing of five movements involving a total of 150 personnel to Albania, Macedonia, Kosovo, Turkey, and Iraq. Training and assessing these personnel prior to their movement resulted in all personnel accomplishing their jobs and returning safely home.

SERVICES TO VETERANS, LOGISTICS, AND SAFETY

While on MedHold at Walter Reed Army Medical Hospital, I interned with the VA and assisted Vets in New Orleans with escaping Hurricane Katrina. I coordinated the relocation of 300+ veterans from the Armed Forces Retirement Home in Gulfport, Mississippi to the U.S. Soldiers' and Airmen's Home located in Washington, D.C. during the aftermath of Hurricane Katrina. Established phone card and clothing rives to ensure that each veteran had sufficient clothing and was able to communicate with their family and friends to ensure they were aware of the veteran's current living arrangements. Awarded the Humanitarian Service Medal and the Mississippi Emergency Service Medal for my actions.

STEP 1

★ **Review the Federal Job Process**

Tens of thousands of federal government jobs are posted on USAJOBS alone every day. Which ones will you apply for? In this step, get off to a running start with your job search by getting answers to the three most important questions.

Which job titles do you qualify for?

On pages 22-31, determine if you qualify for a certain job title or series. You can review the list of major occupations and job series in government. Also be aware that new jobs are created every day with new agencies and missions!

Which agencies are good matches for you?

We recommend that you review the list of agencies on pages 15-20 to determine your top agencies of consideration. This way you can focus your resume toward a particular federal agency mission and service. Excepted service agencies are listed on page 20.

Which grades or salary levels do you qualify for?

Check out pages 32-36 for information on how to determine your grade or salary level by analyzing your education, training, certifications, years of experience, and specialized knowledge. You will learn how to interpret the pay bands that are posted on many vacancy announcements. The pay bands are bands of grades with large ranges of salary.

Use this worksheet to set your federal job search goals.

TARGET AGENCIES

What are your target agencies?

TARGET JOB TITLES AND SERIES

What is your current military job title?

How many years of specialized experience do you have?

Which federal job titles or series seem correct for you?

GRADE AND SALARY

What is your current military rank?

What is your current military salary?

What will be your target federal grade level?

What will your salary be, if you apply to a pay band agency?

★ DETAILS ABOUT YOUR FEDERAL JOB SEARCH

The following questions and answers will provide information concerning any special hiring programs that can offer you faster job consideration.

GENERAL INFORMATION
Name:
U.S. Citizen?   Yes   No
Email:
Home phone:
Work phone:

VETERANS' QUESTIONS
Were you in the military service?   Yes   No
If so, what branch of the service and your highest rank:

Do you know what your Preference is?
Points for Preference:
Period of Military Service:
Retired Military?
For more info about various veterans' federal job benefits: www.opm.gov/veterans

SECURITY CLEARANCE
Do you have a clearance?
Have you ever had a clearance?   Yes   No
If yes, what were the dates?
What type of clearance?

LANGUAGE SKILLS
Foreign languages that you know:

Skill level? Fair, Moderate, Fluent

FOREIGN RESIDENCE / EMPLOYMENT
Have you lived overseas? If so, when and why?

COMPUTER SKILLS
Skill level with computers?
(i.e., personal use, system development, advanced, professional?)

FEDERAL AGENCY PREFERENCE
Agencies you are targeting:

PAST FEDERAL EMPLOYMENT
If you ever held a federal position, write the dates of service, pay plan, series, and grade:

SALARY EXPECTATIONS
What is the LOWEST salary you will accept?

JOB TITLES

List job titles of positions for which you wish to be considered. (i.e., business manager, marketing director, customer services, etc.)

FEDERAL EMPLOYMENT STATUS QUESTIONS

The federal government gives certain people preference (or status) for hiring if they are among these groups:

Are you married to a person in the military?

Are you disabled?

Have you worked for the federal government? If so, are you eligible to be reinstated without competition?

Are you eligible for placement in the federal service based upon your former military service? (i.e., are you eligible for a Veterans Recruitment Appointment?)

EDUCATION

Do you have a degree? If so, what was your major? Graduation date?

Have you just graduated with a 3.5 GPA?

If you do not have a degree yet, what have you been studying?

CERTIFICATION

Do you have any special certifications?

SKILLS

What are your five most significant skills? (computer, writing, speaking, research, etc.)

KNOWLEDGE

What types of knowledge do you have? (real estate, administrative, business, etc.)

INTERESTS

What types of positions interest you? (administration, contracts, finance, accounting, IT, engineering, etc.)

The different classes of jobs in the federal government each have different hiring practices. This information is important for you to strategize your application depending on the job type you are applying for.

Competitive Service Jobs

Competitive Service jobs are under U.S. Office of Personnel Management's (OPM) jurisdiction and follow laws to ensure that applicants and employees receive fair and equal treatment in the hiring process. Selecting officials have broad authority to review more than one applicant source before determining the best-qualified candidate based on job-related criteria. Positions are open to the public. For positions lasting more than 120 days, vacancies must be announced and posted on USAJOBS, the federal government's central repository of job information. Veterans' preference rules are applied. Candidates are ranked and referred in order, i.e., highest scoring candidates or candidates in the highest quality group are referred first for selection. However, compensable disabled veterans "float" to the top, except for scientific and professional upper-level positions.

Excepted Service Jobs

Excepted Service jobs are the jobs with agencies that set their own qualification requirements and are not subject to the appointment, pay, and classification rules in Title 5, United States Code. These agencies are able to be more flexible with recruitment incentives, salaries, promotions, and other personnel matters. They are also subject to veterans' preference. Positions may be in the excepted service by law, executive order, or action of OPM. Excepted service jobs are not required to be posted on USAJOBS. To learn about their job opportunities, you must go to the specific agency websites.

Direct Hire

Agencies use direct hiring when there is a shortage of qualified candidates, or when an agency has a critical hiring need, such as one caused by an emergency or unanticipated events, or changed mission requirements. Direct hire provides a quick way to hire individuals in the competitive service. Although it requires agencies to publicly post their vacancies on USAJOBS, they do not need to apply veterans' preference or rate and rank qualified candidates. Once a qualified candidate is found, agencies may offer the job on the spot and may appoint the candidate immediately. OPM has allowed government-wide use of direct hire for the following occupations: information technology management related to security; x-ray technicians; medical officers, nurses, and pharmacists; and positions involved in Iraqi reconstruction efforts requiring fluency in Arabic.

Pathways

Executive Order 13562, dated December 27, 2010, established a comprehensive structure to help the federal government be more competitive in recruiting and hiring talented individuals who are in school or who have recently received a degree. Student and recent graduate programs are to be consolidated into three clear program paths: internship program, recent graduate program, and the Presidential Management Fellows (PMF) program. Programs will not be in place until final regulations are implemented. In the meantime, the current PMF, SCEP, and STEP programs remain in effect until such time Pathways is complete. The FCIP program has been discontinued.

Check the agencies of your choice.
View entire list at http://www.usa.gov/Agencies/Federal/All_Agencies/index.shtml.

Alphabetical list of organizations in the federal executive, legislative, and judicial branches

A

Administration for Children and Families
Administration on Aging (AOA)
Administration for Community Living
Administrative Office of the U.S. Courts
Advisory Council on Historic Preservation
Agency for Healthcare Research and Quality
Agency for International Development
Agency for Toxic Substances and Disease Registry
Agricultural Marketing Service
Agricultural Research Service
Air Force, Department of
AMTRAK (National Railroad Passenger Corporation)
Animal and Plant Health Inspection Service
Appalachian Regional Commission
Architect of the Capitol
Armed Forces Retirement Home
Arms Control and International Security, Under Secretary for
Army, Department of
Army Corps of Engineers (USACE)

B

Botanic Garden (USBG)
Broadcasting Board of Governors (BBG), (Voice of America, Radio/TV Marti, and more)
Bureau of Alcohol, Tobacco, Firearms, and Explosives (ATF)
Bureau of Economic Analysis
Bureau of Engraving and Printing
Bureau of Indian Affairs
Bureau of Industry and Security
Bureau of International Labor Affairs
Bureau of Labor Statistics
Bureau of Land Management
Bureau of Public Debt
Bureau of Reclamation
Bureau of Transportation Statistics

C

Census Bureau
Center for Nutrition Policy and Promotion
Centers for Disease Control and Prevention (CDC)
Centers for Medicare & Medicaid Services
Central Intelligence Agency (CIA)
Citizenship and Immigration Services Bureau (USCIS)
Civilian Radioactive Waste Management
Coast Guard (USCG)
Commission on Civil Rights
Community Oriented Policing Services
Community Planning and Development
Comptroller of the Currency, Office of the
Congressional Budget Office
Consumer Financial Protection Bureau
Consumer Product Safety Commission (CPSC)
Cooperative State Research, Education, and Extension Service
Corporation for National and Community Service
Council of Economic Advisers
Council on Environmental Quality
Court of Appeals for the Armed Forces
Court of Appeals for the Federal Circuit
Court of Appeals for Veterans Claims
Court of Federal Claims
Court of International Trade
Customs and Border Protection

D

Defense Advanced Research Projects Agency
Defense Commissary Agency
Defense Contract Audit Agency
Defense Contract Management Agency
Defense Finance and Accounting Service

STEP 1

Check the agencies of your choice.

Defense Information Systems Agency
Defense Intelligence Agency (DIA)
Defense Legal Services Agency
Defense Logistics Agency
Defense Nuclear Facilities Safety Board
Defense Security Cooperation Agency
Defense Security Service
Defense Threat Reduction Agency
Department of Agriculture (USDA)
Department of Commerce (DOC)
Department of Defense (DOD)
Department of Education (ED)
Department of Energy (DOE)
Department of Health and Human Services (HHS)
Department of Homeland Security (DHS)
Department of Housing and Urban Development (HUD)
Department of the Interior (DOI)
Department of Justice (DOJ)
Department of Labor (DOL)
Department of State (DOS)
Department of Transportation (DOT)
Department of the Treasury
Department of Veterans Affairs (VA)
Disability Employment Policy, Office of
Drug Enforcement Administration (DEA)

E

Economic and Statistics Administration
Economic, Business and Agricultural Affairs
Economic Development Administration
Economic Research Service
Elementary and Secondary Education, Office of
Employee Benefits Security Administration
Employment and Training Administration
Employment Standards Administration
Energy Efficiency and Renewable Energy
Energy Information Administration
Environmental Management
Environmental Protection Agency (EPA)

Equal Employment Opportunity Commission (EEOC)
Executive Office for Immigration Review

F

Fair Housing and Equal Opportunity, Office of
Faith-Based and Community Initiatives Office
Farm Service Agency (FSA)
Federal Aviation Administration
Federal Bureau of Investigation (FBI)
Federal Bureau of Prisons
Federal Communications Commission (FCC)
Federal Deposit Insurance Corporation (FDIC)
Federal Election Commission (FEC)
Federal Emergency Management Agency (FEMA)
Federal Financing Bank
Federal Highway Administration
Federal Housing Enterprise Oversight
Federal Housing Finance Board
Federal Judicial Center
Federal Labor Relations Authority
Federal Law Enforcement Training Center
Federal Mediation and Conciliation Service
Federal Motor Carrier Safety Administration
Federal Railroad Administration
Federal Reserve System
Federal Trade Commission (FTC)
Federal Transit Administration
Financial Management Service
Fish and Wildlife Service
Food and Drug Administration (FDA)
Food and Nutrition Service
Food Safety and Inspection Service
Foreign Agricultural Service
Forest Service
Fossil Energy

G

Government Accountability Office (GAO)
General Services Administration
Geological Survey (USGS)

Global Affairs
Government National Mortgage Association
Government Printing Office
Grain Inspection, Packers, and Stockyards
    Administration

H

Health Resources and Services Administration
Holocaust Memorial Museum
House of Representatives
House Office of Inspector General
House Office of the Clerk
House Organizations, Commissions, and Task
    Forces

I

Indian Health Service
Industrial College of the Armed Forces
Information Resource Management College
Institute of Museum and Library Services
Internal Revenue Service (IRS)
International Broadcasting Bureau (IBB)
International Trade Administration (ITA)

J

Joint Chiefs of Staff
Joint Forces Staff College
Judicial Circuit Courts of Appeal by Geographic
    Location and Circuit

L

Lead Hazard Control
Legal Services Corporation
Library of Congress

M

Marine Corps
Maritime Administration
Marketing and Regulatory Programs
Marshals Service

Merit Systems Protection Board
Mine Safety and Health Administration
Mineral Management Service
Minority Business Development Agency
Mint
Missile Defense Agency
Multifamily Housing Office

N

National Aeronautics and Space
    Administration (NASA)
National Agricultural Statistics Service
National Archives and Records Administration
    (NARA)
National Capital Planning Commission
National Cemetery Administration
National Communications System
National Council on Disability
National Credit Union Administration
National Defense University
National Drug Intelligence Center
National Endowment for the Arts
National Endowment for the Humanities
National Guard Bureau
National Highway Traffic Safety Administration
National Institute of Standards and Technology
    (NIST)
National Institutes of Health (NIH)
National Labor Relations Board
National Laboratories
National Marine Fisheries
National Mediation Board
National Nuclear Security Administration
National Oceanic and Atmospheric
    Administration (NOAA)
National Park Service
National Science Foundation
National Security Agency/Central Security
    Service
National Technical Information Service
National Telecommunications and Information
    Administration

Check the agencies of your choice.

National Transportation Safety Board (NTSB)
National War College
National Weather Service
Natural Resources Conservation Service
Navy, Department of the
Nuclear Energy, Science and Technology
Nuclear Regulatory Commission
Nuclear Waste Technical Review Board

O

Occupational Safety & Health Administration
    (OSHA)
Office of Government Ethics
Office of Management and Budget (OMB)
Office of National Drug Control Policy
    (ONDCP)
Office of Personnel Management
Office of Science and Technology Policy
Office of Special Counsel
Office of Thrift Supervision
Overseas Private Investment Corporation

P

Pardon Attorney Office
Parole Commission
Patent and Trademark Office
Peace Corps
Pension Benefit Guaranty Corporation
Policy Development and Research
Political Affairs
Postal Rate Commission
Postal Service (USPS)
Postsecondary Education, Office of
Power Marketing Administrations
Presidio Trust
Public Diplomacy and Public Affairs
Public and Indian Housing

R

Radio and TV Marti (Español)
Radio Free Asia (RFA)

Radio Free Europe/Radio Liberty (RFE/RL)
Railroad Retirement Board
Regulatory Information Service Center
Research and Special Programs Administration
Research, Education, and Economics
Risk Management Agency
Rural Business-Cooperative Service
Rural Development
Rural Housing Service
Rural Utilities Service

S

Science Office
Secret Service
Securities and Exchange Commission (SEC)
Selective Service System
Senate
Small Business Administration (SBA)
Smithsonian Institution
Social Security Administration (SSA)
Social Security Advisory Board
Special Education and Rehabilitative Services
Stennis Center for Public Service
Student Financial Assistance Programs
Substance Abuse and Mental Health Services
    Administration
Supreme Court of the United States
Surface Mining, Reclamation, and Enforcement
Surface Transportation Board

T

Tax Court
Technology Administration
Tennessee Valley Authority
Trade and Development Agency
Transportation Security Administration
Trustee Program

U

U.S. International Trade Commission

U.S. Mission to the United Nations
U.S. National Central Bureau – Interpol
U.S. Trade Representative
Unified Combatant Commands
Uniformed Services University of the Health
    Sciences

V

Veterans Benefits Administration
Veterans Employment and Training Service
Veterans Health Administration
Voice of America (VOA)

W

White House
White House Office of Administration
Women's Bureau

★ EXCEPTED SERVICE AGENCIES

These major excepted service departments and agencies do not post their vacancies on USAJOBS:

- Federal Reserve System, Board of Governors
- Central Intelligence Agency
- Defense Intelligence Agency
- U.S. Department of State
- Federal Bureau of Investigation
- General Accounting Office
- Agency for International Development
- National Security Agency
- U.S. Nuclear Regulatory Commission
- Postal Rates Commission
- Postal Service
- Tennessee Valley Authority
- United States Mission to the United Nations

Department of Veterans Affairs, Health Services and Research Administration:
Physicians, Dentists, Nurses, Nurse Anesthetists, Physicians' Assistants, Podiatrists, Optometrists, Expanded-function Dental Auxiliaries, Occupational Therapists, Pharmacists, Licensed Practical/Vocational Nurses, Physical Therapists and Certified/Registered Respiratory Therapists.

Judicial Branch

Legislative Branch

Public International Organizations:

- International Monetary Fund
- Pan American Health Organization
- United Nations Children's Fund
- United Nations Development Program
- United Nations Institute
- United Nations Population Fund
- United Nations Secretariat
- World Bank, International Finance Corporation (IFC) and the Multilateral Investment Guarantee Agency (MIGA)

Find a link to the list of Excepted Service Agencies and Excepted Service Positions at:
www.resume-place.com/resources/useful-links/

Finding Your Job Titles

The government classifies jobs that share common characteristics into general work "groups" and specific "series." The occupations are generally divided into white-collar (General Schedule, or GS) and trades (Wage Grade, or WG) job groups. Use this section to identify possible job fits for your skills and interests.

If you are interested in more detailed information about the work performed by a particular job series, you can research the Position Classification Standards maintained by OPM. The standards and other classification documents are available on OPM's web site, at www.opm.gov/fedclass.

Keep in mind that the classification system explains how a job is assigned a title, occupational series, and grade, and explains the type and level of work done at each grade within an occupation. However, the classification standards do not address how an individual qualifies for a particular job or line of work. Information about qualifications is found in OPM's Qualifications Standards, at www.opm.gov/qualifications.

Carefully reading the qualifications requirements for various occupational series at the different grades will help you make realistic decisions about what jobs to pursue, (title, series, and grade) and may save you from wasting time applying for jobs where you simply don't meet those requirements.

STEP 1

Find your target job titles from this listing of the HANDBOOK OF OCCUPATIONAL GROUPS AND FAMILIES, U.S. Office of Personnel Management Office of Classification, Washington, DC.

GS-000 – MISCELLANEOUS OCCUPATIONS GROUP (NOT ELSEWHERE CLASSIFIED)

This group includes all classes of positions the duties of which are to administer, supervise, or perform work, which cannot be included in other occupational groups either because the duties are unique, or because they are complex and come in part under various groups.

Series in this group are:
GS-006 - Correctional Institution Administration Series
GS-007 - Correctional Officer Series
GS-011 - Bond Sales Promotion Series
GS-018 - Safety and Occupational Health Management Series
GS-019 - Safety Technician Series
GS-020 - Community Planning Series
GS-021 - Community Planning Technician Series
GS-023 - Outdoor Recreation Planning Series
GS-025 - Park Ranger Series
GS-028 - Environmental Protection Specialist Series
GS-029 - Environmental Protection Assistant Series
GS-030 - Sports Specialist Series
GS-050 - Funeral Directing Series
GS-060 - Chaplain Series
GS-062 - Clothing Design Series
GS-072 - Fingerprint Identification Series
GS-080 - Security Administration Series
GS-081 - Fire Protection and Prevention Series
GS-082 - United States Marshal Series
GS-083 - Police Series
GS-084 - Nuclear Materials Courier Series
GS-085 - Security Guard Series
GS-086 - Security Clerical and Assistance Series
GS-090 - Guide Series
GS-095 - Foreign Law Specialist Series
GS-099 - General Student Trainee Series

GS-100 – SOCIAL SCIENCE, PSYCHOLOGY, AND WELFARE GROUP

This group includes all classes of positions the duties of which are to advise on, administer, supervise, or perform research or other professional and scientific work, subordinate technical work, or related clerical work in one or more of the social sciences; in psychology; in social work; in recreational activities; or in the administration of public welfare and insurance programs.

Series in this group are:
GS-101 - Social Science Series
GS-102 - Social Science Aid and Technician Series
GS-105 - Social Insurance Administration Series
GS-106 - Unemployment Insurance Series
GS-107 - Health Insurance Administration Series
GS-110 - Economist Series
GS-119 - Economics Assistant Series
GS-130 - Foreign Affairs Series
GS-131 - International Relations Series
GS-132 - Intelligence Series
GS-134 - Intelligence Aid and Clerk Series
GS-135 - Foreign Agricultural Affairs Series
GS-136 - International Cooperation Series
GS-140 - Manpower Research and Analysis Series
GS-142 - Manpower Development Series
GS-150 - Geography Series
GS-160 - Civil Rights Analysis Series
GS-170 - History Series
GS-180 - Psychology Series
GS-181 - Psychology Aid and Technician Series
GS-184 - Sociology Series
GS-185 - Social Work Series
GS-186 - Social Services Aid and Assistant Series
GS-187 - Social Services Series
GS-188 - Recreation Specialist Series
GS-189 - Recreation Aid and Assistant Series
GS-190 - General Anthropology Series
GS-193 - Archeology Series
GS-199 - Social Science Student Trainee Series

GS-200 – HUMAN RESOURCES MANAGEMENT GROUP

This group includes all classes of positions the duties of which are to advise on, administer, supervise, or perform work involved in the various phases of human resources management.

Series in this group are:
GS-201 - Human Resources Management Series
GS-203 - Human Resources Assistance Series
GS-241 - Mediation Series
GS-243 - Apprenticeship and Training Series
GS-244 - Labor Management Relations Examining Series
GS-260 - Equal Employment Opportunity Series
GS-299 - Human Resources Management Student Trainee Series

GS-300 – GENERAL ADMINISTRATIVE, CLERICAL, AND OFFICE SERVICES GROUP

This group includes all classes of positions the duties of which are to administer, supervise, or perform work involved in management analysis; stenography, typing, correspondence, and secretarial work; mail and file work; the operation of office appliances; the operation of communications equipment, use of codes and ciphers, and procurement of the most effective and efficient communications services; the operation of microform equipment, peripheral equipment, mail processing equipment, duplicating equipment, and copier/duplicating equipment; and other work of a general clerical and administrative nature.

Series in this group are:
GS-301 - Miscellaneous Administration and Program Series
GS-302 - Messenger Series
GS-303 - Miscellaneous Clerk and Assistant Series
GS-304 - Information Receptionist Series
GS-305 - Mail and File Series
GS-309 - Correspondence Clerk Series
GS-312 - Clerk-Stenographer and Reporter Series
GS-313 - Work Unit Supervising Series
GS-318 - Secretary Series
GS-319 - Closed Microphone Reporting Series
GS-322 - Clerk-Typist Series

GS-326 - Office Automation Clerical and Assistance Series
GS-332 - Computer Operation Series
GS-335 - Computer Clerk and Assistant Series
GS-340 - Program Management Series
GS-341 - Administrative Officer Series
GS-342 - Support Services Administration Series
GS-343 - Management and Program Analysis Series
GS-344 - Management and Program Clerical and Assistance Series
GS-346 - Logistics Management Series
GS-350 - Equipment Operator Series
GS-356 - Data Transcriber Series
GS-357 - Coding Series
GS-360 - Equal Opportunity Compliance Series
GS-361 - Equal Opportunity Assistance Series
GS-382 - Telephone Operating Series
GS-390 - Telecommunications Processing Series
GS-391 - Telecommunications Series
GS-392 - General Telecommunications Series
GS-394 - Communications Clerical Series
GS-399 - Administration and Office Support Student Trainee Series

GS-400 – NATURAL RESOURCES MANAGEMENT AND BIOLOGICAL SCIENCES GROUP

This group includes all classes of positions the duties of which are to advise on, administer, supervise, or perform research or other professional and scientific work or subordinate technical work in any of the fields of science concerned with living organisms, their distribution, characteristics, life processes, and adaptations and relations to the environment; the soil, its properties and distribution, and the living organisms growing in or on the soil, and the management, conservation, or utilization thereof for particular purposes or uses.

Series in this group are:
GS-401 - General Natural Resources Management and Biological Sciences Series
GS-403 - Microbiology Series
GS-404 - Biological Science Technician Series
GS-405 - Pharmacology Series
GS-408 - Ecology Series
GS-410 - Zoology Series
GS-413 - Physiology Series
GS-414 - Entomology Series

GS-415 - Toxicology Series
GS-421 - Plant Protection Technician Series
GS-430 - Botany Series
GS-434 - Plant Pathology Series
GS-435 - Plant Physiology Series
GS-437 - Horticulture Series
GS-440 - Genetics Series
GS-454 - Rangeland Management Series
GS-455 - Range Technician Series
GS-457 - Soil Conservation Series
GS-458 - Soil Conservation Technician Series
GS-459 - Irrigation System Operation Series
GS-460 - Forestry Series
GS-462 - Forestry Technician Series
GS-470 - Soil Science Series
GS-471 - Agronomy Series
GS-480 - Fish and Wildlife Administration Series
GS-482 - Fish Biology Series
GS-485 - Wildlife Refuge Management Series
GS-486 - Wildlife Biology Series
GS-487 - Animal Science Series
GS-499 - Biological Science Student Trainee Series

GS-500 – ACCOUNTING AND BUDGET GROUP

This group includes all classes of positions the duties of which are to advise on, administer, supervise, or perform professional, technical, or related clerical work of an accounting, budget administration, related financial management or similar nature.

Series in this group are:
GS-501 - Financial Administration and Program Series
GS-503 - Financial Clerical and Technician Series
GS-505 - Financial Management Series
GS-510 - Accounting Series
GS-511 - Auditing Series
GS-512 - Internal Revenue Agent Series
GS-525 - Accounting Technician Series
GS-526 - Tax Specialist Series
GS-530 - Cash Processing Series
GS-540 - Voucher Examining Series
GS-544 - Civilian Pay Series
GS-545 - Military Pay Series
GS-560 - Budget Analysis Series
GS-561 - Budget Clerical and Assistance Series
GS-592 - Tax Examining Series
GS-593 - Insurance Accounts Series
GS-599 - Financial Management Student Trainee Series

GS-600 – MEDICAL, HOSPITAL, DENTAL, AND PUBLIC HEALTH GROUP

This group includes all classes of positions the duties of which are to advise on, administer, supervise or perform research or other professional and scientific work, subordinate technical work, or related clerical work in the several branches of medicine, surgery, and dentistry or in related patient care services such as dietetics, nursing, occupational therapy, physical therapy, pharmacy, and others.

Series in this group are:
GS-601 - General Health Science Series
GS-602 - Medical Officer Series
GS-603 - Physician's Assistant Series
GS-610 - Nurse Series
GS-620 - Practical Nurse Series
GS-621 - Nursing Assistant Series
GS-622 - Medical Supply Aide and Technician Series
GS-625 - Autopsy Assistant Series
GS-630 - Dietitian and Nutritionist Series
GS-631 - Occupational Therapist Series
GS-633 - Physical Therapist Series
GS-635 - Kinesiotherapy Series
GS-636 - Rehabilitation Therapy Assistant Series
GS-637 - Manual Arts Therapist Series
GS-638 - Recreation/Creative Arts Therapist Series
GS-639 - Educational Therapist Series
GS-640 - Health Aid and Technician Series
GS-642 - Nuclear Medicine Technician Series
GS-644 - Medical Technologist Series
GS-645 - Medical Technician Series
GS-646 - Pathology Technician Series
GS-647 - Diagnostic Radiologic Technologist Series
GS-648 - Therapeutic Radiologic Technologist Series
GS-649 - Medical Instrument Technician Series
GS-650 - Medical Technical Assistant Series
GS-651 - Respiratory Therapist Series
GS-660 - Pharmacist Series
GS-661 - Pharmacy Technician Series
GS-662 - Optometrist Series
GS-664 - Restoration Technician Series
GS-665 - Speech Pathology and Audiology Series
GS-667 - Orthotist and Prosthetist Series
GS-668 - Podiatrist Series
GS-669 - Medical Records Administration Series
GS-670 - Health System Administration Series
GS-671 - Health System Specialist Series
GS-672 - Prosthetic Representative Series

GS-673 - Hospital Housekeeping Management Series
GS-675 - Medical Records Technician Series
GS-679 - Medical Support Assistance Series
GS-680 - Dental Officer Series
GS-681 - Dental Assistant Series
GS-682 - Dental Hygiene Series
GS-683 - Dental Laboratory Aid and Technician Series
GS-685 - Public Health Program Specialist Series
GS-688 - Sanitarian Series
GS-690 - Industrial Hygiene Series
GS-696 - Consumer Safety Series
GS-698 - Environmental Health Technician Series
GS-699 - Medical and Health Student Trainee Series

GS-700 - VETERINARY MEDICAL SCIENCE GROUP

This group includes positions that advise on, administer, supervise, or perform professional or technical support work in the various branches of veterinary medical science.

Series in this group are:
GS-701 - Veterinary Medical Science Series
GS-704 - Animal Health Technician Series
GS-799 - Veterinary Student Trainee Series

GS-800 – ENGINEERING AND ARCHITECTURE GROUP

This group includes all classes of positions the duties of which are to advise on, administer, supervise, or perform professional, scientific, or technical work concerned with engineering or architectural projects, facilities, structures, systems, processes, equipment, devices, materials or methods. Positions in this group require knowledge of the science or art, or both, by which materials, natural resources, and power are made useful.

Series in this group are:
GS-801 - General Engineering Series
GS-802 - Engineering Technician Series
GS-803 - Safety Engineering Series
GS-804 - Fire Protection Engineering Series
GS-806 - Materials Engineering Series
GS-807 - Landscape Architecture Series
GS-808 - Architecture Series
GS-809 - Construction Control Technical Series
GS-810 - Civil Engineering Series
GS-817 - Survey Technical Series

GS-819 - Environmental Engineering Series
GS-828 - Construction Analyst Series
GS-830 - Mechanical Engineering Series
GS-840 - Nuclear Engineering Series
GS-850 - Electrical Engineering Series
GS-854 - Computer Engineering Series
GS-855 - Electronics Engineering Series
GS-856 - Electronics Technical Series
GS-858 - Biomedical Engineering Series
GS-861 - Aerospace Engineering Series
GS-871 - Naval Architecture Series
GS-873 - Marine Survey Technical Series
GS-880 - Mining Engineering Series
GS-881 - Petroleum Engineering Series
GS-890 - Agricultural Engineering Series
GS-892 - Ceramic Engineering Series
GS-893 - Chemical Engineering Series
GS-894 - Welding Engineering Series
GS-895 - Industrial Engineering Technical Series
GS-896 - Industrial Engineering Series
GS-899 - Engineering and Architecture Student Trainee Series

GS-900 – LEGAL AND KINDRED GROUP

This group includes all positions that advise on, administer, supervise, or perform work of a legal or kindred nature.

Series in this group are:
GS-901 - General Legal and Kindred Administration Series
GS-904 - Law Clerk Series
GS-905 - General Attorney Series
GS-920 - Estate Tax Examining Series
GS-930 - Hearings and Appeals Series
GS-945 - Clerk of Court Series
GS-950 - Paralegal Specialist Series
GS-958 - Employee Benefits Law Series
GS-962 - Contact Representative Series
GS-963 - Legal Instruments Examining Series
GS-965 - Land Law Examining Series
GS-967 - Passport and Visa Examining Series
GS-986 - Legal Assistance Series
GS-987 - Tax Law Specialist Series
GS-991 - Workers' Compensation Claims Examining Series
GS-993 - Railroad Retirement Claims Examining Series

GS-996 - Veterans Claims Examining Series
GS-998 - Claims Assistance and Examining Series
GS-999 - Legal Occupations Student Trainee Series

GS-1000 – INFORMATION AND ARTS GROUP

This group includes positions which involve professional, artistic, technical, or clerical work in (1) the communication of information and ideas through verbal, visual, or pictorial means, (2) the collection, custody, presentation, display, and interpretation of art works, cultural objects, and other artifacts, or (3) a branch of fine or applied arts such as industrial design, interior design, or musical composition. Positions in this group require writing, editing, and language ability; artistic skill and ability; knowledge of foreign languages; the ability to evaluate and interpret informational and cultural materials; or the practical application of technical or esthetic principles combined with manual skill and dexterity; or related clerical skills.

Series in this group are:
GS-1001 - General Arts and Information Series
GS-1008 - Interior Design Series
GS-1010 - Exhibits Specialist Series
GS-1015 - Museum Curator Series
GS-1016 - Museum Specialist and Technician Series
GS-1020 - Illustrating Series
GS-1021 - Office Drafting Series
GS-1035 - Public Affairs Series
GS-1040 - Language Specialist Series
GS-1046 - Language Clerical Series
GS-1051 - Music Specialist Series
GS-1054 - Theater Specialist Series
GS-1056 - Art Specialist Series
GS-1060 - Photography Series
GS-1071 - Audiovisual Production Series
GS-1082 - Writing and Editing Series
GS-1083 - Technical Writing and Editing Series
GS-1084 - Visual Information Series
GS-1087 - Editorial Assistance Series
GS-1099 - Information and Arts Student Trainee Series

GS-1100 – BUSINESS AND INDUSTRY GROUP

This group includes all classes of positions the duties of which are to advise on, administer, supervise, or perform work pertaining to and requiring a knowledge of business and trade practices, characteristics and use of equipment, products, or property, or industrial production methods and processes, including the conduct of investigations and studies; the collection, analysis, and dissemination of information; the establishment and maintenance of contacts with industry and commerce; the provision of advisory services; the examination and appraisement of merchandise or property; and the administration of regulatory provisions and controls.

Series in this group are:
GS-1101 - General Business and Industry Series
GS-1102 - Contracting Series
GS-1103 - Industrial Property Management Series
GS-1104 - Property Disposal Series
GS-1105 - Purchasing Series
GS-1106 - Procurement Clerical and Technician Series
GS-1107 - Property Disposal Clerical and Technician Series
GS-1130 - Public Utilities Specialist Series
GS-1140 - Trade Specialist Series
GS-1144 - Commissary Management Series
GS-1145 - Agricultural Program Specialist Series
GS-1146 - Agricultural Marketing Series
GS-1147 - Agricultural Market Reporting Series
GS-1150 - Industrial Specialist Series
GS-1152 - Production Control Series
GS-1160 - Financial Analysis Series
GS-1163 - Insurance Examining Series
GS-1165 - Loan Specialist Series
GS-1169 - Internal Revenue Officer Series
GS-1170 - Realty Series
GS-1171 - Appraising Series
GS-1173 - Housing Management Series
GS-1176 - Building Management Series
GS-1199 - Business and Industry Student Trainee Series

GS-1200 – COPYRIGHT, PATENT, AND TRADEMARK GROUP

This group includes all classes of positions the duties of which are to advise on, administer, supervise, or perform professional scientific, technical, and legal work involved in the cataloging and registration of copyrights, in the classification and issuance of patents, in the registration of trademarks, in the prosecution of applications for patents before the Patent Office, and in the giving of advice to Government officials on patent matters.

Series in this group are:
GS-1202 - Patent Technician Series
GS-1210 - Copyright Series
GS-1220 - Patent Administration Series
GS-1221 - Patent Adviser Series
GS-1222 - Patent Attorney Series
GS-1223 - Patent Classifying Series
GS-1224 - Patent Examining Series
GS-1226 - Design Patent Examining Series
GS-1299 - Copyright and Patent Student Trainee Series

GS-1300 – PHYSICAL SCIENCES GROUP

This group includes all classes of positions the duties of which are to advise on, administer, supervise, or perform research or other professional and scientific work or subordinate technical work in any of the fields of science concerned with matter, energy, physical space, time, nature of physical measurement, and fundamental structural particles; and the nature of the physical environment.

Series in this group are:
GS-1301 - General Physical Science Series
GS-1306 - Health Physics Series
GS-1310 - Physics Series
GS-1311 - Physical Science Technician Series
GS-1313 - Geophysics Series
GS-1315 - Hydrology Series
GS-1316 - Hydrologic Technician Series
GS-1320 - Chemistry Series
GS-1321 - Metallurgy Series
GS-1330 - Astronomy and Space Science Series
GS-1340 - Meteorology Series
GS-1341 - Meteorological Technician Series
GS-1350 - Geology Series
GS-1360 - Oceanography Series
GS-1361 - Navigational Information Series
GS-1370 - Cartography Series
GS-1371 - Cartographic Technician Series
GS-1372 - Geodesy Series
GS-1373 - Land Surveying Series
GS-1374 - Geodetic Technician Series
GS-1380 - Forest Products Technology Series
GS-1382 - Food Technology Series

GS-1384 - Textile Technology Series
GS-1386 - Photographic Technology Series
GS-1397 - Document Analysis Series
GS-1399 - Physical Science Student Trainee Series

GS-1400 – LIBRARY AND ARCHIVES GROUP

This group includes all classes of positions the duties of which are to advise on, administer, supervise, or perform professional and scientific work or subordinate technical work in the various phases of library and archival science.

Series in this group are:
GS-1410 - Librarian Series
GS-1411 - Library Technician Series
GS-1412 - Technical Information Services Series
GS-1420 - Archivist Series
GS-1421 - Archives Technician Series
GS-1499 - Library and Archives Student Trainee Series

GS-1500 – MATHEMATICS AND STATISTICS GROUP

This group includes all classes of positions the duties of which are to advise on, administer, supervise, or perform professional and scientific work or related clerical work in basic mathematical principles, methods, procedures, or relationships, including the development and application of mathematical methods for the investigation and solution of problems; the development and application of statistical theory in the selection, collection, classification, adjustment, analysis, and interpretation of data; the development and application of mathematical, statistical, and financial principles to programs or problems involving life and property risks; and any other professional and scientific or related clerical work requiring primarily and mainly the understanding and use of mathematical theories, methods, and operations.

Series in this group are:
GS-1501 - General Mathematics and Statistics Series
GS-1510 - Actuarial Science Series
GS-1515 - Operations Research Series
GS-1520 - Mathematics Series
GS-1521 - Mathematics Technician Series
GS-1529 - Mathematical Statistics Series

STEP 1

GS-1530 - Statistics Series
GS-1531 - Statistical Assistant Series
GS-1540 - Cryptography Series
GS-1541 - Cryptanalysis Series
GS-1550 - Computer Science Series
GS-1599 - Mathematics and Statistics Student Trainee Series

GS-1600 – EQUIPMENT, FACILITIES, AND SERVICES GROUP

This group includes positions the duties of which are to advise on, manage, or provide instructions and information concerning the operation, maintenance, and use of equipment, shops, buildings, laundries, printing plants, power plants, cemeteries, or other government facilities, or other work involving services provided predominantly by persons in trades, group require technical or managerial knowledge and ability, plus a practical knowledge of trades, crafts, or manual labor operations.

Series in this group are:
GS-1601 - Equipment, Facilities, and Services Series
GS-1603 - Equipment, Facilities, and Services Assistance Series
GS-1630 - Cemetery Administration Services Series
GS-1640 - Facility Operations Services Series
GS-1654 - Printing Services Series
GS-1658 - Laundry Operations Services Series
GS-1667 - Food Services Series
GS-1670 - Equipment Services Series
GS-1699 – Equipment, Facilities, and Services Student Trainee Series

GS-1700 – EDUCATION GROUP

This group includes positions that involve administering, managing, supervising, performing, or supporting education or training work when the paramount requirement of the position is knowledge of, or skill in, education, training, or instruction processes.

Series in this group are:
GS-1701 - General Education and Training Series
GS-1702 - Education and Training Technician Series
GS-1710 - Education and Vocational Training Series
GS-1712 - Training Instruction Series
GS-1715 - Vocational Rehabilitation Series

GS-1720 - Education Program Series
GS-1725 - Public Health Educator Series
GS-1730 - Education Research Series
GS-1740 - Education Services Series
GS-1750 - Instructional Systems Series
GS-1799 - Education Student Trainee Series

GS-1800 – INVESTIGATION GROUP

This group includes all classes of positions the duties of which are to advise on, administer, supervise, or perform investigation, inspection, or enforcement work primarily concerned with alleged or suspected offenses against the laws of the United States, or such work primarily concerned with determining compliance with laws and regulations.

Series in this group are:
GS-1801 - General Inspection, Investigation, and Compliance Series
GS-1802 - Compliance Inspection and Support Series
GS-1810 - General Investigating Series
GS-1811 - Criminal Investigating Series
GS-1812 - Game Law Enforcement Series
GS-1815 - Air Safety Investigating Series
GS-1816 - Immigration Inspection Series
GS-1822 - Mine Safety and Health Series
GS-1825 - Aviation Safety Series
GS-1831 - Securities Compliance Examining Series
GS-1850 - Agricultural Commodity Warehouse Examining Series
GS-1854 - Alcohol, Tobacco and Firearms Inspection Series
GS-1862 - Consumer Safety Inspection Series
GS-1863 - Food Inspection Series
GS-1864 - Public Health Quarantine Inspection Series
GS-1881 - Customs and Border Protection Interdiction Series
GS-1884 - Customs Patrol Officer Series
GS-1889 - Import Specialist Series
GS-1890 - Customs Inspection Series
GS-1894 - Customs Entry and Liquidating Series
GS-1895 - Customs and Border Protection Series
GS-1896 - Border Patrol Agent Series
GS-1897 - Customs Aid Series
GS-1899 - Investigation Student Trainee Series

GS-1900 – QUALITY ASSURANCE, INSPECTION, AND GRADING GROUP

This group includes all classes of positions the duties of which are advise on, supervise, or perform administrative or technical work primarily concerned with the quality assurance or inspection of material, facilities, and processes; or with the grading of commodities under official standards.
Series in this group are:
GS-1910 - Quality Assurance Series
GS-1980 - Agricultural Commodity Grading Series
GS-1981 - Agricultural Commodity Aid Series
GS-1999 - Quality Inspection Student Trainee Series

GS-2000 – SUPPLY GROUP

This group includes positions that involve work concerned with furnishing all types of supplies, equipment, material, property (except real estate), and certain services to components of the federal government, industrial, or other concerns under contract to the government, or receiving supplies from the federal government. Included are positions concerned with one or more aspects of supply activities from initial planning, including requirements analysis and determination, through acquisition, cataloging, storage, distribution, utilization to ultimate issues for consumption or disposal. The work requires a knowledge of one or more elements or parts of a supply system, and/or supply methods, policies, or procedures.

Series in this group are:
GS-2001 - General Supply Series
GS-2003 - Supply Program Management Series
GS-2005 - Supply Clerical and Technician Series
GS-2010 - Inventory Management Series
GS-2030 - Distribution Facilities and Storage Management Series
GS-2032 - Packaging Series
GS-2050 - Supply Cataloging Series
GS-2091 - Sales Store Clerical Series
GS-2099 - Supply Student Trainee Series

GS-2100 – TRANSPORTATION GROUP

This group includes all classes of positions the duties of which are to advise on, administer, supervise, or perform clerical, administrative, or technical work involved in the provision of transportation service to the government, the regulation of transportation utilities by the government, or the management of government-funded transportation programs, including transportation research and development projects.

Series in this group are:
GS-2101 - Transportation Specialist Series
GS-2102 - Transportation Clerk and Assistant Series
GS-2110 - Transportation Industry Analysis Series
GS-2121 - Railroad Safety Series
GS-2123 - Motor Carrier Safety Series
GS-2125 - Highway Safety Series
GS-2130 - Traffic Management Series
GS-2131 - Freight Rate Series
GS-2135 - Transportation Loss and Damage Claims Examining Series
GS-2144 - Cargo Scheduling Series
GS-2150 - Transportation Operations Series
GS-2151 - Dispatching Series
GS-2152 - Air Traffic Control Series
GS-2154 - Air Traffic Assistance Series
GS-2161 - Marine Cargo Series
GS-2181 - Aircraft Operation Series
GS-2183 - Air Navigation Series
GS-2185 - Aircrew Technician Series
Gs-2199 - Transportation Student Trainee Series

GS-2200 – INFORMATION TECHNOLOGY GROUP

Series in this group are:
GS-2210 - Information Technology Management Series
GS-2299 - Information Technology Student Trainee

★ WHICH JOB TITLES ARE CORRECT FOR YOU?

Trades, Craft, and Labor Positions
www.opm.gov/fedclass/html/fwseries.asp

Federal Classification and Job Grading Systems

- ▸ Main
- ▸ White Collar Positions
  - ↳ Position Classification Standards
  - ↳ Functional Guides

- ▸ Trades, Craft, and Labor Positions
  - ↳ Job Grading Standards
  - ↳ Functional Standards

- ▸ Draft Standards
- ▸ Recent Issuances
- ▸ Classification Guidance

RELATED LINKS

- ▸ Classification Appeals
- ▸ Compensation Administration
- ▸ General Schedule Qualifications
- ▸ Trades and Labor Occupation Qualifications

Job Grading Standards for Trades, Craft, and Labor Positions

Job grading standards provide information used in determining the occupational series and title of jobs performing trades, craft, and labor work in the Federal Government. They also provide grading criteria for positions classified under the Federal Wage System (FWS).

If a series is not included in this list, we have not issued a specific job grading standard for that series. Documents on the Classifying Trades, Craft, and Labor Positions webpage provide series definitions and guidance on classifying jobs in series with no published standard.

Series	Occupational Group
2500	Wire Communications Equipment Installation and Maintenance Group
2600	Electronic Equipment Installation and Maintenance Group
2800	Electrical Installation and Maintenance Group
3100	Fabric and Leather Work Group
3300	Instrument Work Group
3400	Machine Tool Work Group
3500	General Services and Support Work Group
3600	Structural and Finishing Work Group
3700	Metal Processing Group
3800	Metal Work Group
3900	Motion Picture, Radio, Television, and Sound Equipment Operating Group
4100	Painting and Paperhanging Group
4200	Plumbing and Pipefitting Group
4300	Pliable Materials Work Group
4400	Printing Group
4600	Wood Work Group
4700	General Maintenance and Operations Work Group
4800	General Equipment Maintenance Group
5000	Plant and Animal Work Group
5200	Miscellaneous Occupations Group

Trades, Craft, and Labor Positions cont.

2500 Wire Communications Equipment Installation and Maintenance Group
2600 Electronic Equipment Installation and Maintenance Group
2800 Electrical Installation and Maintenance Group
3100 Fabric and Leather Work Group
3300 Instrument Work Group
3400 Machine Tool Work Group
3500 General Services and Support Work Group
3600 Structural and Finishing Work Group
3700 Metal Processing Group
3800 Metal Work Group
3900 Motion Picture, Radio, Television, Sound Equipment Operation Group
4100 Painting and Paperhanging Group
4200 Plumbing and Pipefitting Group
4300 Pliable Materials Work Group
4400 Printing Group
4600 Wood Work Group
4700 General Maintenance and Operations Work Group
4800 General Equipment Maintenance Group
5000 Plant and Animal Work Group
5200 Miscellaneous Occupations Group
5300 Industrial Equipment Maintenance Group
5400 Industrial Equipment Operation Group
5700 Transportation/Mobile Equipment Operation Group
5800 Transportation/Mobile Equipment Maintenance Group
6500 Ammunition, Explosives, and Toxic Materials Work Group
6600 Armament Work Group
6900 Warehousing and Stock Handling Group
7000 Packing and Processing Group
7300 Laundry, Dry Cleaning, and Pressing Group
7400 Food Preparation and Serving Group
7600 Personal Services Group
8200 Fluid Systems Maintenance Group
8600 Engine Overhaul Group
8800 Aircraft Overhaul Group

Effective January 2012 – Annual Rates by Grade and Step

www.opm.gov/oca/12tables/html/gs.asp

Grade	Step 1	Step 2	Step 3	Step 4	Step 5	Step 6	Step 7	Step 8	Step 9	Step 10	Within Grade
1	17803	18398	18990	19579	20171	20519	21104	21694	21717	22269	VARIES
2	20017	20493	21155	21717	21961	22607	23253	23899	24545	25191	VARIES
3	21840	22568	23296	24024	24752	25480	26208	26936	27664	28392	728
4	24518	25335	26152	26969	27786	28603	29420	30237	31054	31871	817
5	27431	28345	29259	30173	31087	32001	32915	33829	34743	35657	914
6	30577	31596	32615	33634	34653	35672	36691	37710	38729	39748	1019
7	33979	35112	36245	37378	38511	39644	40777	41910	43043	44176	1133
8	37631	38885	40139	41393	42647	43901	45155	46409	47663	48917	1254
9	41563	42948	44333	45718	47103	48488	49873	51258	52643	54028	1385
10	45771	47297	48823	50349	51875	53401	54927	56453	57979	59505	1526
11	50287	51963	53639	55315	56991	58667	60343	62019	63695	65371	1676
12	60274	62283	64292	66301	68310	70319	72328	74337	76346	78355	2009
13	71674	74063	76452	78841	81230	83619	86008	88397	90786	93175	2389
14	84697	87520	90343	93166	95989	98812	101635	104458	107281	110104	2823
15	99628	102949	106270	109591	112912	116233	119554	122875	126196	129517	3321

Now that we have covered the basic general schedule grade and pay system, we'll tell you that not every agency follows this pay system anymore. "Pay banding," which allows an organization to combine two or more grades into a wider "band," is an increasingly popular alternative to the traditional GS system. The "grade" information for jobs in agencies using pay banding will have a different look, and that look may be specific to a particular agency. Don't be surprised to see something as odd as ZP-1 or NO-2 in place of GS-5 or GS-7. Focus on the duties, the salary, whether you are qualified for the job, and whether you would like to have it. Remember, the federal government is large, and needs a way to increase flexibility of pay based on performance. Pay bands are its answer.

Example of Pay Band Salaries: Transportation Security Administration

www.tsa.gov/join/careers/pay_scales.shtm

Pay Band	Minimum	Maximum
A	$17,083	$24,977
B	$19,570	$28,546
C	$22,167	$33,303
D	$25,518	$38,277
E	$29,302	$44,007
F	$33,627	$50,494
G	$39,358	$60,982
H	$48,007	$74,390
I	$58,495	$90,717
J	$71,364	$110,612
K	$85,311	$132,237
L	$101,962	$155,500
M	$120,236	$155,500

FIND YOUR GRADE AND SALARY

The actual salary that the agency offers will be dependent on your qualifications. The general qualifications needed to receive that pay (and equivalent GS grade) is determined by the grade of the position. Please see the announcement for specific education and experience requirements for the position.

Salary Range (based on the 2012 pay schedule)	Qualifications Requirements
$20,000 – 35,600	High school with no experience (for GS-2) to one year of specialized experience at the GS-4 level, or four years of education beyond high school (for GS-5).
$27,400 – 44,000	Three years of general experience or one year of specialized experience or a bachelor's degree (for GS-5) or one year of graduate work or superior academic achievement as an undergraduate (for GS-7).
$40,000 – 65,400	Masters degree or equivalent or one year of specialized experience equal to GS-7 (for GS-9) or Ph.D. or equivalent or one year of specialized experience equal to GS-9 (for GS-11).
$60,000 – 129,500	One year of specialized experience equal to experience at the next lower grade (GS 12 through 15).

NOTE: In 2012, locality pay can increase the above ranges by 4.72 to 35.15 percent.

Qualifying Based on Education Alone

GS-2: High school graduation or equivalent (i.e., GED)

GS-3: One year above high school

GS-4: Two years above high school (or Associate's degree)

GS-5: Bachelor's degree

GS 7: One full year of graduate study or Bachelor's degree with superior academic achievement (GPA 2.95 or higher out of a possible 4.0)

GS-9: Master's degree or equivalent such as J.D. or LL.B.

GS-11: Ph.D.

NOTE: There are exceptions to this chart; there are occupations that will not accept education in lieu of experience.

Military Rank to U.S. Federal Civilian Grades and Pay

You can use this chart below to estimate the federal grade equivalents for military rank. However, there is no one-to-one grade equivalent between the General Schedule and the military grading system. HR specialists rate applications based on the experience described in your resume. It is, therefore, important to describe your experience to a degree of detail that clearly portrays the level of responsibilities you had, the complexity of your work, the supervision you received, the guidelines you followed, and the impact of your work. Also, remember that volunteer work for which you received little or no pay is given the same credit as comparable paid experience.

Federal Civilian Grade—General Schedule	Federal Civilian Grade—Wage System	Military—Commissioned Officer (Army/Air Force/ UMSC, then Navy/Coast Guard ranks)	Military—Warrant Officer	Military--Enlisted
GS-01				E-1
GS-02				E-3
GS-03	WG 1-8			E-4
GS-04	WG 9-11			E-4
GS-05	WL 1-5			E-4/5
GS-06	WS 1-7			
GS-07		O-1 Second Lieutenant or Ensign	WO-1	E-5
GS-08				
GS-09	WG 12-15	O-2 First Lieutenant or Lieutenant (Junior Grade)	CWO-2	E-5/7
GS-10	WS 8-13			
	WL 6-14			
GS-11		O-3 Captain or Lieutenant	CWO-3	E-9
GS-12		O-4 Major or Lieutenant Commander	CWO-4	
GS-13	WS 14-19	O-4 or 5 Lieutenant Colonel/Major or Commander/Lieutenant Commander	CWO-5	
GS-14	WL-15	O-5 Lieutenant Colonel or Commander		
GS-15		O-6 Colonel or Captain		
SES or equivalent		O-7 Brigadier General or Rear Admiral (Lower Half) O-8 Major General or Rear Admiral (Upper Half) O-9 Lieutenant General or Vice Admiral O-10 General or Admiral		

The human resources staffing specialist will detemine your qualifications for the position by looking at the following items in your federal resume. Qualification determinations are based on:

EDUCATION

➤ Major field of study
➤ # of years completed or # of semester hours completed
➤ GPA

TRAINING

➤ Related to job
➤ # of days or hours

EXPERIENCE

➤ Quality of experience
  • Directly related to the job or general nature of work
  • Complexity of assignments (what, for whom, why)
  • Decision-making authority or span of control
  • Knowledge, skills, and abilities used
➤ Length of experience
  • Full-time or part-time
  • # of hours per week

PATCO

Federal jobs are made up of the following basic categories, titles, and grades:

Professional – GS-5 through 15

Professional positions, such as chemists, accountants, doctors, social workers, and psychologists, have a positive educational requirement. They must be educated and certified by a board or institution.

Administrative – GS-5 through 15

These jobs usually have the title of Analyst or Specialist. Administrative jobs do not require a degree. You can qualify for an Administrative (Analyst or Specialist) position based on specialized experience, education, or both. Certain law enforcement positions are in this category: Special Agent, Border Patrol, Customs Inspector, Immigration Inspector.

Technical – GS-6 through 12

These jobs are the Technician or Assistant positions. Some job titles are Accounting Technicians or Assistants. There is no educational requirement. The main requirement is experience. The Federal Aviation Administration Electronics Technician can be classified as high as a GS-12. Bachelor's degree graduates can qualify for Technician or Assistant positions starting at GS-7 with superior academic achievement.

Clerical – GS-1 through 5

These jobs are Clerk positions. There is no educational requirement.
An Associate of Arts degree graduate will qualify for GS-3 or GS-4 positions.

Other

Law enforcement professionals (not special agents), including security guards, police, rangers, park rangers, and U.S. Marshals; blue collar and other professions not covered in other categories.

Are you or your spouse eligible for any special preferences or do you or your spouse belong to any special group of people? How about other members of your household?

For Everyone

Direct Hire

Agencies use direct hire authority when there is a shortage of qualified candidates (i.e., an agency is unable to identify qualified candidates despite extensive recruitment or extended announcement periods), or when an agency has a critical hiring need, such as an emergency or unanticipated event, or changed mission requirements. Its very nature allows agencies to forgo rating and ranking qualified candidates or applying veterans' preference.

Direct hire provides agencies a quick way to hire individuals in the competitive service. Positions filled through direct hire are posted on USAJOBS.

Certain agencies have direct hire authority for certain occupations. However, OPM allows the government-wide use of direct hire authority for the following occupations:

- Information technology management related to security
- X-ray technicians
- Medical officers, nurses, and pharmacists
- Positions involved in Iraqi reconstruction efforts that require fluency in Arabic
- Acquisition positions covered under title 41 (effective through September 30, 2012)

Pathways

An Executive Order 13562 dated December 27, 2010 established a comprehensive structure to help the federal government be more competitive in recruiting and hiring talented individuals who are in school or who have recently received a degree. The executive order directs the consolidation of student and recent graduate programs into the Pathways Programs framework with three clear program paths tailored to recruit, train, and retain well-qualified candidates.

Programs will not be in place until final regulations to implement them become effective following an opportunity for public comment. Comments are now in, and implementation is expected to occur during the summer of 2012. Current PMF, SCEP, and STEP programs remain in effect until such time Pathways regulations are promulgated.

The Pathways program will include a/an:

- Internship Program: Targets students enrolled in a wide variety of educational institutions
- Recent Graduate Program: Targets recent graduates of trade and vocational schools, community colleges, universities, and other qualifying institutions. Students must apply within two years of graduation. Successful graduates will be placed in a two year career development program and later considered for noncompetitive conversion to career jobs.

Schedule A Hiring Program—Individuals with Disabilities, Including Veterans With 10-Point Preference

Abstracted from http://www.opm.gov/disability/mngr_3-13.asp

What it provides: Federal agencies fill jobs two ways, competitively and noncompetitively. Persons with disabilities may apply for jobs filled either way. Jobs filled competitively are advertised through vacancy announcements. Jobs that are filled noncompetitively do not have to be advertised. Instead, a selecting official can select a person with a disability who has a Schedule A certification and is qualified for the job. People who are selected for jobs must meet the qualification requirements for the jobs and be able to perform the essential duties of the jobs with or without reasonable accommodation.

When it is used: People who are disabled and have a certification letter from a State Vocational Rehabilitation Office or the Department of Veterans Affairs may apply for noncompetitive appointment through the Schedule A hiring authority. Applicants with certification letters may apply directly to agencies' Selective Placement Program Coordinators or their equivalent to be considered for jobs. Managers can contact the agency's Selective Placement Program Coordinator or human resources office or their equivalent to obtain more information about sources for applicants with disabilities. A link to OPM's directory of Selective Placement Program Coordinators by agency is listed at the bottom of this page.

Who is eligible: The Federal Government has special appointing authorities for persons with disabilities. To be eligible for these noncompetitive, Schedule A appointments, a person must meet the definition for being disabled. The person must have a severe physical, cognitive, or emotional disability; have a history of having such disability; or be perceived as having such disability. In addition, the person must obtain a certification letter from a State Vocational Rehabilitation Office or the Department of Veterans Affairs to be eligible for appointment under these special authorities.

Disabled veterans may also be considered under special hiring programs for disabled veterans with disability ratings from the Department of Veterans Affairs of 30% or more. Managers and supervisors can contact the agency's human resources office or Selective Placement Program Coordinator or their equivalent to obtain more information on appointment authorities.

Tips for Veterans Waiting for Disability Rating from Veterans Affairs

Vets can apply for the Schedule A through the local State's Vocational Rehabilitation (DORS in MD and through the country) program, even though they are Vets and should receive their services through the VA VRE program. But veterans can also apply to their state VR first to get some assistance and get the ball rolling. The State VR can make connection(s) to the Veteran's VRE program. The State Vocational Rehabilitation Counselor can provide a Schedule A for a veteran who is disabled and waiting for the disability rating from the VA.

For more information:
- http://apps.opm.gov/sppc_directory/
- golearn.gov/HiringReform/index.htm

For Veterans

Veterans Recruitment Appointment (VRA) (Formerly Veterans Readjustment Appointment)

What it provides: VRA allows appointment of eligible veterans up to GS-11 or equivalent. Veterans are hired under excepted appointments to positions that are otherwise in the competitive service. After the individual satisfactorily completes two years of service, the veteran must be converted noncompetitively to a career or career-conditional appointment.

When it is used: VRA is used for filling entry-level to mid-level positions.

Who is eligible: VRA eligibility applies to the following veterans:
- Disabled veterans;
- Veterans who served on active duty in the Armed Forces during a war declared by Congress, or in a campaign or expedition for which a campaign badge has been authorized;
- Veterans who, while serving on active duty in the Armed Forces, participated in a military operation for which the Armed Forces Service Medal was awarded; and
- Veterans separated from active duty within three years.

30 Percent or More Disabled Veterans

What it provides: This authority enables a hiring manager to appoint an eligible candidate to any position for which he or she is qualified, without competition. Unlike the VRA, there's no grade-level limitation. Initial appointments are time-limited appointment of at least 60 days; however, the manager can noncompetitively convert the individual to permanent status at any time during the time-limited appointment.

When it is used: This authority is a good tool for filling positions at any grade level quickly.

Who is eligible: Eligibility applies to the following categories:
- Disabled veterans who were retired from active military service with a disability rating of 30 percent or more; and
- Disabled veterans rated by the Dept. of Veterans Affairs (VA) (within the preceding year) as having a compensable service-connected disability of 30% or more.

Veterans Employment Opportunities Act of 1998 (VEOA)

What it provides: This gives eligible veterans access to jobs otherwise available only to status employees. Veterans are not accorded preference as a factor but are allowed to compete for job opportunities that are not offered to other external candidates. A VEOA eligible who is selected will be given a career or career-conditional appointment.

When it is used: Agencies may appoint VEOA eligibles who have competed under agency merit promotion announcements when they are recruiting from outside their workforce.

Who is eligible: VEOA eligibility applies to the following categories of veterans:
- Preference eligibles; and
- Service personnel separated after three or more years of continuous active service performed under honorable conditions.

For Spouses and Other Family Members

For more detail about the programs listed below for spouses and family members, you can download the entire article from Resume Place website at www.resume-place.com/pdfs/ Spouse Preference Article Jan 2010.pdf.

Military Spouse Employment Preference (MSP)

What it provides: MSP provides priority in the employment selection process for military spouses who are relocating as a result of their military spouse's PCS. Spouse preference may be used for most vacant positions in DoD and applies only within the commuting area of the permanent duty station of the sponsor. Spouses may apply for MSP as early as 30 days prior to your reporting date at the new duty station.

When it is used: 1) Placements into competitive civil service vacancies in the 50 states, the Territories, the Possessions, and the District of Columbia; 2) Employment in foreign areas; 3) Nonappropriated Fund (NAF) employment; 4) Noncompetitive appointments in the civil service for spouses of certain members of the armed forces.

Who is eligible: This preference does not apply to separation or retirement moves. Spouses must be found best qualified for the position and may exercise preference no more than one time per permanent relocation of the sponsor. (If you accept a position with time limitations, i.e., temporary, term, intermittent, or NAF with flexible work schedules, you do not lose your MSP.)

Noncompetitive Appointment of Certain Military Spouses

What it provides: As of 9/11/09, federal agencies were granted the authority to hire "qualified" military spouses without going through the competitive process. Spouses can find out about job opportunities by going to USAJOBS or websites of specific agencies.

When it is used: The use of this authority is discretionary by federal agencies and the hiring managers. The authority is not limited to specific positions or grade levels, but spouses must meet the same requirements as other applicants, to include qualification requirements. Spouses are not provided any "hiring preference" nor does it create an entitlement to federal jobs over other qualified applicants. It is the applicant's responsibility to apply for a job and request consideration for employment under this authority as a military spouse.

Who is eligible:
- Spouses of service members serving on PCS for 180 days or more (provided the spouse relocates to the member's new permanent duty station)
- Spouses of retired service members (who retired under Chapter 61, Title 10, USA), with a disability rating of 100% at the time of retirement
- Spouses of former service members who retired or were released and have a 100% disability rating from the VA
- Un-remarried widows or widowers of armed forces members killed while serving on active duty.

DoD Military Spouse Preference Program (PPP) Program S

Abstracted from Chapter 14 of the DOD Priority Placement Program (PPP) Handbook

What it provides: The latest military spouse appointment authority, Executive Order 13473, allows military spouses who have never worked for the government to register in the PPP, if they were married and placed on their sponsor's PCS orders prior to his/her PCS to the new duty station. You can Google E.O. 13473 to find out more about this military spouse appointment eligibility.

When it is used: A spouse may register at the losing A-coded activity up to 30 days prior to the sponsor's reporting date, or upon relocation, at any A-coded activity in the commuting area of the sponsor's new duty station. Eligible program S registrants must be considered as military spouse preference candidates when referred through Program S for positions being filled through competitive merit promotion procedures. They are eligible for spouse preference if they rank among the Best Qualified (BQ).

Who is eligible: Registration in Program S is limited to spouses of active duty military members of the U.S. Armed Services (including the U.S. Coast Guard and full-time National Guard). Also, with certain exceptions, the spouse may register only if he or she accompanies a military sponsor who is:

a. Assigned by Permanent Change of Station (PCS) move from overseas to U.S. or to a different commuting area within the U.S., including the U.S. territories or possessions;

b. Relocating to a new and permanent duty station after completing basic and advanced individual training;

c. Permanently assigned to the same duty station where initial entry training was received.

Other Requirements: The marriage to the sponsor must have occurred prior to the sponsor's reporting date to the new duty station.

Why the Program S Military spouse PPP Program is a good idea!

See a true Spouse Program S PPP example: Natalie Richardson's sample in this book!

> "Good morning Kathryn! Any military spouse can get PPP if they apply for it within 30 days of a military move/PCS. All I had to do was call the CPAC office (civilian personnel advisory center) and make an appoint to "get" PPP. They evaluated my resume and gave me a GS-score BASED on my resume. Once I was in the system, I was told to apply on USAJOBS to whatever jobs I was good for. In the meantime, if they found a job on USAJOBs, they would "recommend" it to me. I would have a certain amount of time to apply; if I didn't at least apply, then I would be dropped from PPP. Once I accepted a job, I was pushed out of the PPP program. If it wasn't for your resume, I wouldn't have received a high GS score. If it wasn't for PPP, I wouldn't have gotten a job as fast as I did." -- *Natalie Richardson*

For more information: DOD PPP Handbook, Read Chapter 14 for Military Spouse PPP, Updated July 2011, www.cpms.osd.mil/care/care_ppp.aspx

STEP 1

Derived Veterans' Preference

What it provides: By law, veterans who are disabled or who served on active duty in the Armed Forces during certain specified time periods or in military campaigns are entitled to preference over others in competitive external hiring. When a veteran is not able to use his or her federal employment preference, then the preference can essentially "pass on" to his or her spouse, widow, or mother. The eligible applicant receives an additional 10 points to a passing examination score or rating.

When it is used: This preference is based on service of a veteran who is not able to use the federal employment preference. This authority is not related to the MSP described above.

Who is eligible: Spouses, widows, widowers, or mothers of veterans who are unable to work as a result of their service-related disability or have died while on active duty. Both a mother and a spouse (including widow or widower) may be entitled to preference on the basis of the same veteran's service if they both meet the requirements. However, neither may receive preference if the veteran is living and is qualified for federal employment.

Military Spouses Internship Program

For a limited number of positions through the end of FY2010, federal agencies can hire a military spouse and DoD will pay for one year of salary, benefits, and training.

More information: www.cpms.osd.mil/milspouse/milspouse_index.aspx

---

The Veterans Opportunity to Work (VOW) (Public Law 112-56) was enacted on November 21, 2011, requiring federal agencies to treat certain active duty service members as preference eligibles, even if the service members have not yet been discharged or released from active duty.

Many members of the armed forces start their civilian job search prior to discharge or release from active duty and do not have a DD-214 when applying for federal jobs. The VOW Act serves to ensure these individuals do not lose the opportunity to be considered for federal service (and awarded their veterans' preference entitlements if applicable) despite not having a DD-214 to submit along with their resumes. **In lieu of the DD-214, veterans and preference eligibles can submit other written documentation from the armed forces certifying that the service member is expected to be discharged or released from active duty service in the armed forces under honorable conditions not later than 120 days after the date the certification is signed.**

Summarized from:
www.chcoc.gov/transmittals/TransmittalDetails.aspx?TransmittalID=4881
Visit this website for more information about the VOW.

Veterans Have Great Tuition, Book, and Housing Benefits for Going to College

For their service to America, veterans earn valuable education benefits. These programs are for active duty military, separated or retired veterans, and spouses and children of military. Service members can use the benefits while on active duty or after active duty. In order to be 100% eligible for the Post-9/11 GI Bill, a veteran must have served at least 36 months that were not obligated service time to any other benefit (such as attending one of the academies or the loan repayment program). A veteran can take advantage of Post-9/11 GI Bill benefits prior to the 36-month mark at lower rates. For example, after 90 days of service, the veteran would be eligible at 40%. The percentage of maximum benefit payable increases with the length of active duty, up to 36 months at 100%.

If a veteran needs education, training, or certification to begin a new career, then tuition, housing, and books can be fully covered—up to $52,000 for 36 months of covered college tuition plus housing and books. Typically, the GI Bill will pay for the most expensive public institution in any state. For private colleges, the VA has a national cap of $17,500. However, if the school participates in the Yellow Ribbon program, undergraduate students could be eligible for up to $52,000.

Extra Funding Through the Yellow Ribbon Program

The Yellow Ribbon program can provide additional funding for college tuition if the tuition is higher than the Post-9/11 GI Bill tuition cap. The Yellow Ribbon is a yearly contract between the Department of Veterans Affairs and an individual school that elects to participate. More information about the Yellow Ribbon Program is available by phone at the Department of Veterans Affairs, on the Department of Veterans Affairs website, or directly from the participating school. A list of Yellow Ribbon participating institutions is available at http://gibill.va.gov/benefits/post_911_gibill/yellow_ribbon_program.html.

Timing is everything. If a service member wants to transfer his or her benefit to a dependent, that service member must assign the benefit while still on active duty. The GI Bill tuition benefit, or portions of the 36 months, can be assigned to a spouse or children.

More Tuition Benefits Information

Additional places where service members and veterans can learn more about tuition benefits:

- Military base education office
- Selected college's veteran's representative at http://gibill.va.gov

STEP 2

★ **Network–Who Do You Know?**

Why Network?

The U.S. federal government employs nearly two million people in civilian jobs, making it the biggest employer in the country. Understandably, the hiring system can sometimes be complex and daunting. Networking is a great opportunity to learn about the federal hiring system. Other people, especially current and former federal employees, are often the best source of basic information and insider tips.

Who Do You Know and Why Is It Important?

Do you know a supervisor at an agency or a military base? It's possible that veterans could get hired by this supervisor. The Veterans Recruitment Act (VRA) offers special hiring programs for retiring and separating military (disabled or non-disabled). VRA gives supervisors the authority to make direct hires in the case of veterans, but even under direct hiring, the jobseeker must submit an application.

Contact List

Make a list of federal employee contacts and keep their information handy for networking.

Name of person:

Agency where he/she works:

Location:

Job title:

What does he/she do in the government?

The best opportunity for a direct hire is a military job fair. Job fairs are held frequently. On occasion, the federal human resources specialists will bring along actual positions in the government. If you can find a military job fair where agencies are present, it is very possible that you could be given a job offer on the spot! Of course, your chances increase astronomically if you are well-prepared. Take the time to understand federal employment, how to qualify, how to write a federal resume, and how to present your skills professionally. Have your resume ready to hand out. Also, practice the job fair script before you go.

Job Fair Script

Prepare your own job fair script here. Practice your script with a friend.

Hello, my name is: _____

Where are you from? _____

Military service: _____
_____

Recent activity: _____
What was involved in that? _____
What was the result of that activity? _____
What was your role? _____

What kind of job are you looking for? _____
_____
_____

What are your basic skills? _____
_____
_____

Where do you want to live now? _____
_____
_____

STEP 2

JOHN W. SMITH

Walter Reed Army Medical Center
Malogne House Bldg.20, Room 181
6900 Georgia Ave., NW
Washington, DC 20307
Phone: (202) 888-8888
Citizenship: United States of America

Permanent Address:
120 CR 546
Ripley, MS 21228
email: johnsmith@yahoo.com

Veterans' Preference: 10-point, E-4, Mississippi Army National Guard, 2001 to present, Recipient of Purple Heart

SKILLS AND JOB OBJECTIVES:

Team Leader
Law Enforcement
Special Projects

Veteran's Benefits Counselor and Advocate
Emergency Management Coordination
Communications

PROFESSIONAL EXPERIENCE:

Intern, Congressman Gene Taylor – 4th Congressional District of Mississippi
2311 Rayburn House Office Building
Washington, DC 20515-2405
Supervisor: Harry Hoffman (202) 222-5555

August 2005 - Present
Salary: N/A
Supervisor may be contacted

While recuperating and completing physical therapy for injuries sustained as an escort Military Policeman in Iraqi Freedom, served as an Intern for Congressman Gene Taylor.

- ADMINISTRATIVE ASSISTANT: Tasks included word processing, managing files and records, producing reports, designing forms, and other office procedures. Researched and produced reports on veteran's benefits activities. Corresponded with veterans.

- CONSTITUENT SERVICES: Provided customer and personal services to veterans concerning benefits and programs following injuries.

- VETERANS' BENEFITS RESEARCH: Researched TRICARE health insurance issues for national guardsmen and reservists while not on active duty. Advocated for veterans' benefits and provided information to representatives of the Department of Veterans' Affairs. Wrote summaries of veterans' problems and situations concerning processes and service treatment while being transferred from Walter Reed Army Medical Center to outlying regional centers.

JOHN W. SMITH, page two

Accomplishments:

- **Hurricane Katrina / Veterans Home Coordinator**: Coordinated the relocation of 300+ veterans from the Armed Forces Retirement Home in Gulfport, Mississippi to the U.S. Soldiers' and Airmen's Home located in Washington DC during the aftermath of Hurricane Katrina. Established phone card and clothing drives to ensure that each veteran had sufficient clothing and was able to contact family and friends concerning their whereabouts. <u>Awarded the Humanitarian Service Medal and the Mississippi Emergency Service Medal for my actions</u>.

Military Police, Mississippi Army National Guard

155th Separate Armored Brigade   July 2003 - Present
2924 HWY 51 South, Canton, MS 21042   Salary: $21,000/year
Supervisor: Capt. Stephen McCarthy (333) 888-8888   Supervisor may be contacted

- LEAD MILITARY PATROL AND LAW ENFORCEMENT: Lead military police patrol. Coordinate compound and work projects, preserve military control.
- TRAINER AND COORDINATOR: Train law enforcement personnel.
- TRAFFIC ACCIDENT INVESTIGATOR
- PHYSICAL SECURITY
- CIVIL DISTURBANCE AND RIOT CONTROL OPERATIONS

Manufacturing/Operations/Production

Ashley Furniture Factory   2002 - 2004
15900 State Highway 15 North, Ripley, MS 38663

- MANUFACTURING OPERATIONS MANAGEMENT
- CUSTOMER SERVICE AND PROBLEM-SOLVING

Equipment Operator/Supervisor

Pressmen Impact, Inc., New Haven, MS   1995 - 2003

- SUPERVISOR IN GOVERNMENT CONTRACTOR MANUFACTURING FIRM: Supervised custom impact extrusions serving aviation and military needs.
- TRAINED EQUIPMENT OPERATORS in safety and operations.
- EQUIPMENT OPERATIONS: Operated vehicles, forklifts and heavy machinery.

EDUCATION: Rydell High School, Rydell, Mississippi 37771, Graduated 1991
                 Mississippi Community College, Boonsboro, MS 38882
                 Major: Criminal Justice and Social Work, Semester Hours: 56 hours

LICENSE: Commercial Drivers License (Class A)

AWARDS: Army Commendation Medal, Iraq Campaign Medal, Global War on Terrorism, Expeditionary Medal, Purple Heart, Humanitarian Service Medal, Mississippi Emergency Service Medal, National Defense Service Medal, Army Service Ribbon, Armed Forces Reserve Medal

STEP 2

ANESHA T. GAFFNEY

PSC 999 Box 11, Rota, Spain, FPO, AE, 09634
666.666.6666
Email: anesha.gaffney@yahoo.com

Spouse Preference: Family Member of USN Active Duty
Eligible for Consideration under Executive Order 13473, September 11, 2009,
Non-competitive Appointment for Certain Military Spouses

SUMMARY OF SKILLS:

Instructor, Adult Educator
Program Developer and Coordinator
Mentor and Coach, Community Liaison
Administration, Writing and Computer Skills
Public Speaker and Speaking Coach

HIGHLIGHTS OF EXPERIENCE:

- *Family readiness and quality of life support:* career advisor, relocation counselor, and referrals for needed services for USN family members in Rota.
- *Provided adult education, instruction, and training* at University of West Florida, and increased operational readiness.
- *Coordinated and supervised* first Annual Northwest Florida Districts High School Speech Tournament.
- *Community liaison* establishing a network for the University of West Florida and N.A.S. Pensacola.
- *President's Award for Leadership and Diversity,* Univ. of W. FL (2008).
- *Proficient in Microsoft Office programs,* Windows Movie Maker, Final Cut Pro, and iMovie. *Typing Speed 60 wpm.*

WORK EXPERIENCE:

Fleet and Family Support Center, US Navy, Rota, Spain
Volunteer, 8/2010 – Present, 20 hours per week

• INFORMATION AND REFERRAL: Identified and clarified issues or concerns and determined appropriate referral services for military members, retirees, and family members. Ensured customer service and satisfaction.
• CUSTOMER SERVICE: Primary contact for department and ensured and delivered services to customers including educating clients on Relocation Services and Career Resource Development.
• MARKETING: Gathered data for Fleet and Family Support Center and updated information for department calendar and for NAVSTA Rota advertisement.
• DATA GATHERING: Utilized Microsoft Office software to compile and report information and statistics for use at the installation.

University of West Florida, Tampa, FL

Graduate Assistant Coach, 8/2008 to 5/2010, 30 hours per week

• INSTRUCTOR AND COACH. Designed training structure and determined appropriate alternative routes to more effective coaching techniques.
-- Over 5,000 hours of coaching students in effective writing and presentation skills.

• RECRUITER. Made recommendations for University of West Florida Forensics Team. Community liaison for team.
-- Created promotional DVDs; coordinated external events on campus to recruit on-campus students. Coordinated with Director of Forensics with national and regional travel plans for approximately 10 students.

EDUCATION:

Master of Science, Public Administration, 2010
University of West Florida, Pensacola, FL
Financial Management, Public Budgeting
Public Service Human Resources Management
Conflict Management & Resolution, Marketing Management

Bachelor of Arts in Organizational Communications, 2008
University of West Florida, Pensacola, FL

- Leadership Communications (Project Car-A-Van) - raised funds to purchase 15-passenger van for Ronald McDonald House of Northwest Florida (2006).
- Health Communications (Project KidCare) - Worked with Florida KidCare to raise awareness of medical insurance to families of lower socioeconomic status (2008).

HONORS

- Outstanding Graduate Student Award, University of West Florida (2010) Recipient of Letter of Appreciation from Commanding Officer for Volunteer Service, N.A.S. Pensacola (2009)
- President's Award for Leadership and Diversity, University of West Florida (2008)
- Four-time National Finalist: 2008 Pi Kappa Delta National Speech and Debate Championship Finalist (2005-2008)
- Top 24 collegiate speaker in the US in multiple categories, National Forensic Association (2008)
- Volunteer Shining Star Award, Ronald McDonald House of Northwest Florida (2007)

★ LINKEDIN NETWORKING

Life is about relationships, and LinkedIn has opened the door to help build more relationships worldwide.

LinkedIn, with 161 million professionals in its network, is THE business channel for recruiting. However, it is also so much more. LinkedIn provides an opportunity to build a worldwide network of professionals who can assist you with your career. Not only does it work for military to civilian transitions, it also works within the military framework where military to military assignments are concerned. Many military members have made connections for their next military assignment with another military professional using LinkedIn. LinkedIn can be regarded as a marvelous "networking" tool, though it should not be used as a substitute for good old fashioned relationship building.

LinkedIn is a great tool for military spouses for PCS moves. Before LinkedIn, it was very difficult to build a professional network outside of your current assignment. With the worldwide network that LinkedIn provides, military spouses are now able to build a professional network online.

Whether it is a short notice PCS move, a change in PCS orders, or a normal PCS rotation, or even in the case of a service member's extended or remote tours of duty (deployment etc.), military spouses can build strong professional networks via LinkedIn.

Fast updates to your network (and their network) for frequent moves! With the ability of LinkedIn to share the same message with 50 of your contacts at a click of the button, it will not take long to inform your entire contact list of any changes in your business and professional circumstance. Each of your contacts will also have other contacts who will be able to refer you to positions, whether you are simply looking for a change or moving due to a military assignment.

Employers expect to find professionals on LinkedIn. Many of our clients report that their LinkedIn profile was reviewed prior to their interview by the interviewers. This situation works fabulously both ways. The interviewer will have a great impression of you if you have done your work on LinkedIn, and you can research the interviewer prior to your interview.

The LinkedIn resume for Natalie Richardson on the facing page was developed based on her federal resume. We added an exciting profile with her most outstanding skills. LinkedIn is a professional place where you can post a photograph and introduce your strengths, mission, and career history to an employer or network. You can even ask for testimonials from your best customers or team members who will write about your strengths and accomplishments.

Did You Know?

Business professionals and human resources managers use LinkedIn to check out potential job candidates.

Individuals with more than 20 connections are **34 times** more likely to be approached with a job opportunity.

Natalie Richardson Edit

Public Affairs Specialist at US Army

Catonsville, Maryland | Military

Edit Photo

Post an update

Current	**Public Affairs Specialist** at **US Army Reserves** Edit
	+ Add a current position
Past	PARTNER/MANAGER at BaseCouponConnection.com
	MANAGER at Business Card Wholesalers
	PUBLIC RELATIONS at Multi-Care Health and Rehab
	see all ▾
Education	DeKalb Technical Institute
Recommendations	+ Ask for a recommendation
Connections	**1** connection
Websites	+ Add a website
Twitter	+ Add a Twitter account
Public Profile	http://www.linkedin.com/pub/natalie-richardson/52/9b3/b0b Edit

🔁 Share	📄 PDF	🖨 Print

NEW **Add sections** to reflect achievements and experiences on your profile.   ✛ **Add sections**

Summary Edit

Is your company looking for a Public Relations Specialist experienced in Military Affairs? Do you need somebody who can shape the message of your organization to reach new audiences? I am your public affairs specialist!

"Send It To Your Sweetie" Program took off! I founded and ran a successful marketing program for military families who had loved ones in Iraq. This unique program offered free services to military families with members in Iraq for shipping, phone messages, and personal delivery of gifts for their loved ones. I also liaised with base command to insure all regulations and policies were met.

My expertise includes:
- Entrepreneurial spirit and creativity
- Communications and liaison
- Writing and marketing strategies
- Community relations
- Caring for military families and veterans

STEP 2

Experience

+ Add a position

Public Affairs Specialist Edit
US Army Reserves

February 2012 – Present (5 months) | Norfolk, Virginia Area

Successfully landed excellent GS-9 Public Affairs Specialist in charge of all advertising for recruiting program.

Ask for recommendations

PARTNER/MANAGER Edit
BaseCouponConnection.com

September 2010 – February 2011 (6 months) | Fort Stewart, GA

MARKETING PROGRAM FOR MILITARY FAMILIES WITH FAMILY MEMBER IN IRAQ. Developed, owned, managed and operated business that sold marketing contracts to local businesses. Marketed "Send It To Your Sweetie" program targeting free services to military families with members in Iraq for shipping, phone messages, and personal delivery of gifts for their loved ones. Met with base command to ensure all regulations and policies were met.

• Accomplishment: Conceptualized a successful program for family members to send gifts and messages to military personnel. More than 2,500 messages were sent through this program in just six months. Sold business in less than 6 months for a substantial profit.

COMMUNICATIONS. Wrote business plan and developed all aspects of advertising and marketing. Performed cold calls on business customers and followed up with written proposals. Created and delivered PowerPoint presentations to groups of various sizes. Organized and prepared mailings to families and businesses.

WEBSITE DESIGN: Designed website and prepared spreadsheet to track monthly views and clicks. Due to volume of business, interviewed and hired 3 contractors to assist with billing, designing ads, and updating website.

Ask for recommendations

MANAGER Edit
Business Card Wholesalers

June 2005 – July 2009 (4 years 2 months) | Conyers, GA

CREATIVE PRODUCTION: Sold and created full-color, personalized business cards to small businesses. Planned and organized work; efficiently and effectively processed the sale, design, ordering and delivery of product. Ensured quality control, and timeliness for re-orders.

• Established a successful in-home business with local producers of business cards. Contracted with more than 15 vendors and tracked orders for more than 200 customers in two years. Efficiently set up and managed own schedule and schedule for automatic reordering.

CUSTOMER SERVICES: Provided administrative support to customers and vendors. Prepared and sent invoices, collected. Conducted all aspects of accounting.

COMMUNICATION: Corresponded with clients by email and phone, ensured correct grammar, spelling and format. Made cold calls on small businesses – utilized interpersonal skills to develop customer base of 300 businesses within 6 months.

COMPUTER SKILLS: : Utilized typing speed of 45 wpm, Microsoft Suite programs for reports and communication, as well as Photoshop, Illustrator and Corel software to design cards.

Demonstrated strong customer services skills; multi-tasked and worked under pressure and constant deadlines. Maintained customer relations; photographed clients and worked with customers to achieve their desired customized product.

Ask for recommendations

PUBLIC RELATIONS Edit
Multi-Care Health and Rehab
February 2004 – January 2005 (1 year) | Conyers, GA

BUSINESS DEVELOPMENT AND COMMUNICATIONS: Represented chiropractic clinic public relations, made new business contacts, mended old contacts. Developed lasting business relationships with store managers, district managers and their assistants both inside and outside the office. Scheduled health screenings involving blood pressure, glucose and cholesterol testing. Ensured excellent service. Successfully increased patient roster by an average of 5 new patients per week.

Ask for recommendations

STORE MANAGER Edit
Phoebe's Boutique
April 2002 – February 2004 (1 year 11 months) | Lithonia, GA

ADMINISTRATION: Performed office and store administration including management of files and official records, training, payroll and reporting. Communicated effectively orally and in writing. Developed, wrote, standardized and regulated customer service procedures, policies and systems.

COMMUNICATIONS: Communicated with diverse customers, vendors, management to increase sales and resolve problems. Greeted and assisted customers with special requests. Trained staff to deliver excellent customer service.

COMPUTER SKILLS: Utilized computer skills to design website and regulate maintenance for user effectiveness. Used Microsoft Word for correspondence and Excel for reports. Ensured accuracy, correct grammar, spelling, punctuation and syntax.

MANAGED STAFF AND BUDGET: Planned and organized work for sales staff; managed budgeting for cost effective sales planning, directed all tasks and aspects of controlling, maintaining and rotating inventory. Designed store layout and product presentations.

MARKETING SOLUTIONS: Gathered pertinent data, and recognized solutions to initiate and conduct successful storewide marketing campaigns. Controlled and minimized expenses to maximize profit through selected business improvements.

Ask for recommendations

The best way to understand where you fit in government is to search for jobs that fit your experience and interests. Federal vacancy announcements (job advertisements) contain all of the information you need to compare your background to the position requirements.

Types of Federal Job Openings

When you are searching for a federal job, it is helpful to know that there are generally four types of vacancies.

Competitive Service jobs are posted on USAJOBS.

Excepted Service Agencies are not required to post jobs on USAJOBS.

Excepted Service Positions are jobs which also do not have to be posted on USAJOBS.

Find a link to the list of Excepted Service Agencies and Excepted Service Positions at www.resume-place.com/resources/useful-links/.

Agencies can also make Direct Hires for critical need positions or in situations where there are a shortage of candidates. All direct hire authority positions must be posted on USAJOBS. For a list of current direct hire authority positions, visit www.opm.gov/hr_practitioners/lawsregulations/appointingauthorities/index.asp#directhire.

Types of Federal Appointments

Competitive

- Jobs are posted publicly and candidates compete with each other

Non-competitive

- Jobs are not required to be posted publicly
- Jobs may be critical or high-need
- People with certain preferences can get jobs directly, without competing

About 20,000 job announcements are posted on USAJOBS (www.usajobs.gov) every day! Learn how to search effectively and efficiently to locate the vacancy announcements that are best for you.

Search by Keyword and Geographic Location

This is the easiest search to perform and will return a large number of results.

- Go to the USAJOBS home page.

- Enter keywords and geographic location.

- Try to use keyword specific to your unique skill set or the correct job title in quotation marks.

Search by Occupational Family

Once you have seen the range of jobs available in your area, you can start narrowing down the results by searching for jobs within the occupational group that your targeted job falls under. This is an effective strategy, because unless you are expert at federal job titles, you may be qualified for more job titles than you think.

- Go to Advanced Search.

- Search by occupational group by entering the first two numbers of the group.

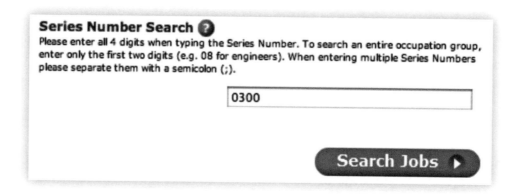

Filtering Your Search Results

- Select geography, pay, or occupational series by using the filters in Advanced Search

- Under "Refine Your Results," current federal employees *and veterans* can select "Jobs for Federal Employees."

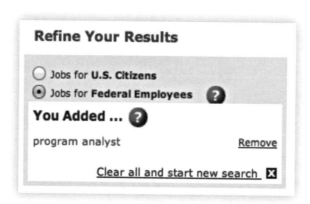

> **Follow the Directions!**
> The following items are the most important elements of a vacancy announcement. Be sure to study each of these items on every announcement so that you follow the directions successfully.

Job, Grade, and Geographic Location

Make sure it's correct for you.

Closing Date

If an announcement reads, "Open Continously" or "Inventory Building", or has a closing date that is two years away, then this announcement is a database-building announcement. If the announcement has specific open and close dates, check if your application has to be received or postmarked by the closing date. If the announcement has already closed, but you are a compensably disabled veteran, call the HR office and ask how you can submit your late application. If you are applying online in a resume builder, try to apply one day early in case there are complications.

Who Can Apply

This is very important. You should only apply to positions where you can qualify. You will see the following notes in this sections:

- Open to Anyone

- All U.S. Citizens

- Status Only (this means current federal employees, reinstatement federal employees, veterans, spouses with noncompetitive applicants, or persons with disabilities)

Location/Duty Station

Make sure you are willing to work in this geographic location. Check the announcement to see if people can apply who live outside the geographic region of the position.

Knowledge, Skills, and Abilities

Read the announcement to see if they list KSAs. They are to be eliminated in the near future, so, if KSAs are listed, you might need to include them in the federal resume instead of on separate sheets of paper.

Questionnaires

Check to see if the announcement requires completion of a questionnaire. In these "assessment questionnaires," you choose your level of skill and experience for each question. You may need to provide examples to demonstrate your experience.

STEP 3

Duties

The description of duties will be written based on the actual position description. The write-up will include "keywords" that should be included in a federal resume.

Qualifications

Are you qualified? Read the qualifications to determine if you have the general and specialized qualifications. If the announcement states one year, that means 52 weeks, 40 hours per week.

General experience is experience that will demonstrate your ability to acquire the particular knowledge and skills for the job. Qualifying general experience will vary in its degree of specificity from one job to another. For some, any progressively responsible work experience may be qualifying. Others may require experience that provided a familiarity with the subject matter or processes of the job. For example, an entry level accounting technician position may require general experience that provided a basic knowledge of debit and credit.

Specialized experience is typically required for positions above the entry level where applicants must have demonstrated that they possess the ability to perform successfully the duties of a position after a normal orientation period. Specialized experience is typically in or related to the work of the postion to be filled. For example, to meet the specialized experience requirements for an accounting technican responsible for maintaining accounts receivable, the applicant would likely be required to have a specific level of experience performing duties such as sending monthly bills, receiving payments, and maintaining accounts receivable ledgers.

How to Apply

Carefully read the "how to apply" instructions as they will differ from agency to agency. The usual application includes a resume, KSAs (if requested separately), last performance evaluation (if possible), DD-214 (if you were in the military), and transcripts (if requested or if you are applying based on education).

SPECIALIZED EXPERIENCE

is usually defined as "one year specialized experience" that is similar to the position in the announcement. This section of an announcement is very important for federal resume writers. The announcement will often say, "Examples include," then suggest examples. Your federal resume MUST cover this specialized experience somewhere in the work experience. Your example does NOT have to be from your most recent position; it can be from any point in your work history, but preferably from the last 10 years.

Overview	Duties	Qualifications & Evaluations	Benefits & Other Info	How to Apply

U.S. DEPARTMENT OF THE INTERIOR
Bureau of Land Management

Job Title: Administrative Officer
Department: Department Of The Interior
Agency: Bureau of Land Management
Job Announcement Number: UT Merit-2012-0134

> This is a permanent position, but be sure to check that you will accept temp and term positions in your USAJOBS profile.

SALARY RANGE:	$47,448.00 to $74,628.00 / Per Year
OPEN PERIOD:	Friday, June 15, 2012 to Friday, June 29, 2012
SERIES & GRADE:	GS-0341-09/11
POSITION INFORMATION:	Permanent, - Full-time
PROMOTION POTENTIAL:	11
DUTY LOCATIONS:	1 vacancy(s) in the following locations: Salt Lake City, UT, US View Map
WHO MAY BE CONSIDERED:	All current or former federal employees with competitive/reinstatement eligibility and Veteran Employment Opportunity Act (VEOA) eligibles. ICTAP/CTAP eligibles within the local commuting area. Persons eligible under Special Hiring Authorities.

JOB SUMMARY:

BLM is seeking a dynamic and energetic individual to join the team as an Administrative Officer.

The BLM manages more land - approximately 253 million acres - than any other Federal agency. This land, known as the National System of Public Lands, is primarily located in 12 Western states, including Alaska. The Bureau, with a budget of about $1 billion, also administers 700 million acres of sub-surface mineral estates throughout the nation. The BLM's multiple-use mission is to sustain the health and productivity of the public lands for the use and enjoyment of present and future generations.

Explore a new career with the BLM - where our people are our greatest natural resource. For additional information about the BLM, visit Our website.

The position is located in Salt Lake City, UT. Information about Salt Lake City and the Salt Lake area can be found at Salt Lake City, Utah

> Check out the mission to see if there are keywords you can use.

KEY REQUIREMENTS

- U.S. Citizenship is required.
- Security Clearance/Background Investigation is required.
- Be sure to read the "How to Apply" and "Required Documents" Sections
- You cannot hold an active real estate license; nor can you have an
- interest or hold stocks in firms with interest in Federal Lands.
- Direct Deposit Required.

DUTIES: Back to top

- The Administrative Officer (AO) is a key supervisor serving the West Desert District Support Services Division.
- Functional responsibilities include budget, procurement, collections and billing, front desk, mail, record management, property and fleet, fire business management and District-side coordination for IT/Telecom and personnel.
- Significant coordination is required within the District in support of the District budget, six direct report staff, two Field Offices and a large dispersed fire organization.
- This position reports to the Assistant District Manager, Support Services.

QUALIFICATIONS REQUIRED:

> Look for keywords in the Duties and Qualifications sections.

Back to top

Specialized Experience Requirements :

In order to be rated as qualified for this position, we must be able to determine that you meet the specialized experience requirement. Include this information in your resume. To be creditable, this experience must have been equivalent in difficulty and complexity to the next lower grade of the position to be filled.

For GS-9: One year of specialized experience equivalent to GS-07 in the Federal service. At the GS-07 level, assignments are significantly more difficult and complex than typically performed by recent graduates of a baccalaureate program. Examples: analyze and evaluate effectiveness of program operations in meeting goals and objectives, recommend or advise on staffing levels, business and management practices to improve organizational efficiencies. OR

A Masters Degree in a field related to business, finance or management or two (2) years of graduate education leading to a master's degree, or equivalent graduate degree in a field related to business, finance or management. Provide a copy of your college transcript(s). OR

An equivalent combination of the specialized experience and graduate education described above. Provide a copy of your college transcripts(s).

For GS-11: One year of specialized experience at the GS-09 level in the Federal service. Examples: Supervisory skills and experience in personnel recruitment and retention; budget and finance oversight experience to include budget formulation, tracking and auditing skills; procurement experience; multiple unit property and fleet experience; fire business experience; records management or oversight. OR

A Ph.D. or equivalent doctoral degree or have successfully completed three (3) full years of progressively higher level graduate education leading to such a degree. Provide a copy of your college transcript(s). OR

An equivalent combination of graduate level education and specialized experience at the GS-09 level (as defined in this vacancy announcement). Provide a copy of your college transcript(s).

> Make sure to cover the "One Year Specialized Experience" requirements in your resume.

You must meet all qualification requirements within 30 days of the closing date. Federal employees in the competitive service also are subject to the Time-In-Grade requirement.

HOW YOU WILL BE EVALUATED:

Upon receipt of your complete application package, a review of your application will be made to ensure you meet the basic qualification requirements. Your rating will be based on your responses to the Job Specific Questionnaire and the information stated in your resume. If qualified, your score may range from 70-100 points. In addition, interviews may be conducted for this position. The interviews may be conducted on a pass/fail basis or may be scored. The job specific questions relate to the following knowledge, skills and abilities required to do the work of this position:

*Skill in establishing programmatic priorities and implementing process improvement across a wide range of administrative support functions.

*Knowledge of leadership and supervision principles and practices regarding employee staffing, training and performance.

*Ability to conduct budget planning and execution to include controlling expenditures.

*Knowledge of federal procurement methods

*Knowledge of property and fleet management practices.

> These knowledge, skills, and abilities should be covered in your resume.

To preview questions please click here.

BENEFITS:

Back to top

To explore the major benefits offered to most Federal employees, visit the Office of Personnel Management's website at Federal Benefits at USAJOBS

> This announcement is a USAJOBS / Application Manager combo application.
>
> The Assessment Questionnaire could contain keywords.

STEP 3

OTHER INFORMATION:

Travel and relocation expenses will be paid consistent with the Federal Travel Regulations and Departmental policy. The use of a relocation service company and home marketing incentive will not be offered. To view FAQ regarding PCS click Here

May require completion of a one (1) year probationary period.

Supervisory Probationary Period: If you are selected for this position, you will be required to serve a one year supervisory/managerial probationary period, if one has not previously been completed.

Before entering on duty, you will be required to complete a Confidential Financial Disclosure Report, OGE-450. You will need to provide the information annually.

Occasional travel may be required.
SELECTIVE SERVICE: Male applicants born after December 31, 1959, must certify that they have registered with the Selective Service System, or are exempt from having to do so under the Selective Service Law. To register or verify your registration go to the Selective Service System website.

Career Transition Assistance Plan (CTAP)/Interagency Career Transition Assistance Program (ICTAP): CTAP provides eligible surplus and displaced Federal competitive service employees with selection priority over other candidates for competitive service vacancies. Information about CTAP/ICTAP eligibility is available from OPM's Career Transition Resources website at CTAP or ICTAP. If your agency has notified you in writing that you are a surplus or displaced employee eligible for CTAP consideration or that you are a displaced employee eligible for ICTAP consideration, you may receive selection priority if: 1) This vacancy is within your CTAP/ICTAP eligibility; 2) You apply under the instructions in this announcement; and 3) You are found well-qualified for this vacancy. You must provide proof of eligibility with your application to receive selection priority. Such proof may include a copy of your written notification of CTAP/ICTAP eligibility, or a copy of your separation personnel action form.

CTAP and ICTAP eligibles will be considered well qualified if they receive a minimum score of 90 based on the rating criteria used for this position.

HOW TO APPLY:

Back to top

To receive consideration for this position, you must provide a complete Application Package, which includes ALL of the following items:

1. Your resume;

2. Your responses to the Assessment Questionnaire;

3. Applicable supporting documents specified in the Required Documents section of this job announcement.

Click on the button "Apply Online" and login to MY USAJOBS. If you haven't already registered with USAJOBS, the system will require you to create a user name and password, complete a questionnaire and paste or type a resume into USAJOBS. If you have already registered with USAJOBS and forgot your login information, select the "Did you forget your username and/or password" link from the right side menu.

If you need assistance in applying on-line, please contact HR at (801) 539-4188 or mpeshell@blm.gov. If applying on-line poses a hardship for you (i.e. you do not have access to the internet) you must contact us prior to the closing date of the announcement for an alternative method of applying.

REQUIRED DOCUMENTS:

In addition to the on-line application (resume and responses to the questionnaire), you are required to submit the following forms:

1. Copy of your recent (non award) SF-50, Notification of Personnel Action, that verifies tenure (block 24, code 1 or 2) and Competitive Status (block 34, code 1).

2. If this applies to you: Copy of Transcripts that include hours and grades from an accredited U.S. college/university. If your degree is from a Foreign Institution See Foreign Education.

3. Veterans' Preference: If you are entitled to veterans' preference, you should indicate the level of veterans' preference you are claiming on your resume. Your veterans' preference entitlement will be verified by the employing agency using the documents you provide.

   For 5-point veterans' preference, please provide your DD-214 (Certificate of Release or Discharge from Active Duty), official statement of service from your command if you are currently on active duty, or other official documentation (e.g., documentation of receipt of a campaign badge or expeditionary medal) that proves your military service was performed under honorable conditions.

   For 10-point veterans' preference, please submit a Standard Form (SF) 15, Application for 10-Point Veteran Preference, DD-214, and the required documentation.

For more information on which type of preference is applicable please visit VetGuide

> Be sure to find and upload your documents early in your federal job search process.

4. Career Transition Assistance Program (CTAP) or Interagency Career Transition Assistance Program (ICTAP) eligibles: documentation verifying your CTAP/ICTAP eligibility. This includes a copy of the agency notice and your most recent SF-50 noting current position, grade level and duty location.

5. If you are applying for this position based on eligibility under other noncompetitive special appointing authorities, you MUST submit proof of this eligibility.

You may submit your documents either via Auto-Requested Fax or by uploading your documents from your USAJOBS Profile.

Auto-Requested Fax: allows you to submit required documentation that will be electronically displayed along with your resume.

UPLOADING DOCUMENTS: instead of faxing your documents you may use the uploading procedures thru Applicant Manager. Do not use both options.

Hard copy paper supplemental documents, submitted without prior Human Resources approval, will be considered as an incomplete application.

Your application package and required documentation must be submitted by 11:59 p.m. Eastern Time by the closing date of this announcement.

AGENCY CONTACT INFO:

Melodee Peshell
Phone: 801-539-4188
Fax: 571-258-4052
Email: mpeshell@blm.gov

Agency Information:
Bureau of Land Management
Utah State Office (UT953mp)
PO Box 45155
440 West 200 South
Salt Lake City, UT
84145
US
Fax: 571-258-4052

> You can contact the human resources specialist listed in the announcement if you have questions.

WHAT TO EXPECT NEXT:

You will be notified of the status of your application as the qualification review process is conducted. You may also check the status of your application by viewing your MY USAJOBs account.

Back to top

< Back to Results

> Be sure to check your Application Status to find out what happened with your application.

The USAJOBS vacancy announcement will have a link to view the Assessment Questionnaire (part 2 of your application) in Application Manager:

HOW TO APPLY: Back to top

To apply for this position, you must provide a complete Application Package which includes:
- Completed Resume – (Required) For more information click on "How To Prepare A Resume"
- Completed Questionnaire – (Required)
- Other supporting documentation as required. Please see the required documents section to determine if there are other documents you are required to submit.

To preview the questionnaire, please go to View Assessment Questions

---

Sample Assessment Questionnaire in Application Manager:

LEVEL DESCRIPTIONS

A- I have not had education, training or experience in performing this task.
B- I have had education or training in performing the task, but have not yet performed it on the job.
C- I have performed this task on the job. My work on this task was monitored closely by a supervisor or senior employee to ensure compliance with proper procedures.
D- I have performed this task as a regular part of a job. I have performed it independently and normally without review by a supervisor or senior employee.
E- I am considered an expert in performing this task. I have supervised performance of this task or I am normally the person who is consulted by other workers to assist them in doing this task because of my expertise.

3. Uses the FAR and DFAR to evaluate sources, negotiate prices and award procurements.

4. Makes purchases involving commercial requirements.

5. Makes non-competitive open market purchases.

6. Makes competitive open market purchases for repeat vendors.

7. Evaluate sources, negotiate and award procurements.

8. Awards purchase orders for supplies.

9. Reviews purchase order provisions to determine regulatory compliance or to improve competition.

10. Maintains purchase order logs, purchase order files and reference materials.

11. Utilizes a Federal contracting/procurement system to process solicitations, awards and/or modifications.

12. Performs market research, identifies potential vendors and creates the solicitation package.

13. Evaluates offers, conduct price analysis for reasonableness and recommends award to the Contracting Officer.

14. Identifies the circumstances prohibiting contract modification.

15. Prepares contract modification using proper procedures and in accordance with existing regulations.

16. Researches applicable contact clauses and provisions for purchases that involve special handling then determine the best method of delivery.

17. Reviews past performance, identifies potential vendors and creates solicitation packages.

18. Perform pre-solicitation review and planning, including review of previous history and the procurement package to ensure completeness and readiness for procurement action.

19. Performs market research to determine availability of the product or producers.

20. Perform evaluation of quotes or offers received.

21. Prepares Contractor Performance History Requests; interprets responses to determine any need for pre-award survey, and prepares Purchase Order or Contract Award documentation.

22. Identifies Purchase Requests for any of the following requirements: small business determination, first article test, government furnished property, or pre-award surveys.

23. Performs evaluation of offers, comparative price analysis for reasonableness and recommends award.

24. Analyzes, develops, and solicits requests for quotations (RFQ) from local and non-local commercial vendors.

> Give yourself all the credit that you can when selecting your multiple choice answers.
>
> Cover these knowledge, skills, and abilities in your federal resume.

STEP 4
★ Analyze Your Core Competencies

Besides specialized experience, education, and technical skills, what "value-added" competencies can you offer a supervisor?

What are competencies?

They are the characteristics affecting performance and are broader than the well-known KSAs (knowledge, skills, and abilities).

Examples

- Are you a team leader who listens to team members' ideas, resolves problems quickly, strives to meet timelines, creates effective plans for training and execution, and gains cooperation and consensus during a project?

- Are you an IT specialist who, in addition to performing all the technical elements of the job, talks to customers about their IT problems, requests, and needs? Are you creative in coming up with solutions to problems?

- Are you an administrative professional who is customer-focused, follows up on inquiries, responds efficiently and effectively, and cares about the dilemmas that customers face?

Which Agencies Use Core Competencies?

The Veterans Administration, Office of Personnel Management, U.S. Marine Corps, Defense Finance & Accounting Service, and many other federal agencies are looking for qualified and skilled applicants who are also skilled in certain core competencies.

How Do I Use Core Competencies When Applying for Jobs?

These characteristics go above and beyond skills. You can stand out in a government resume, question/essay narrative, or behavior-based interview by highlighting these competencies. Study this step and determine the top five or ten competencies that make you a stand-out employee in your field of work. Add these competencies to your resume in the work experience descriptions for a stronger federal resume!

Veterans Administration Competencies

Find your core competencies and check them off the list. Add a few of these competencies into the "duties" section of your work experience.

Interpersonal Effectiveness
- ❑ Builds and sustains positive relationships.
- ❑ Handles conflicts and negotiations effectively.
- ❑ Builds and sustains trust and respect.
- ❑ Collaborates and works well with others.
- ❑ Shows sensitivity and compassion for others.
- ❑ Encourages shared decision-making.
- ❑ Recognizes and uses ideas of others.
- ❑ Communicates clearly, both orally and in writing.
- ❑ Listens actively to others.
- ❑ Honors commitments and promises.

Customer Service
- ❑ Understands that customer service is essential to achieving our mission.
- ❑ Understands and meets the needs of internal customers.
- ❑ Manages customer complaints and concerns effectively and promptly.
- ❑ Designs work processes and systems that are responsive to customers.
- ❑ Ensures that daily work and the strategic direction are customer-centered.
- ❑ Uses customer feedback data in planning and providing products and services.
- ❑ Encourages and empowers subordinates to meet or exceed customer needs and expectations.
- ❑ Identifies and rewards behaviors that enhance customer satisfaction.

Flexibility/Adaptability
- ❑ Responds appropriately to new or changing situations.
- ❑ Handles multiple inputs and tasks simultaneously.
- ❑ Seeks and welcomes the ideas of others.
- ❑ Works well with all levels and types of people.
- ❑ Accommodates new situations and realities.
- ❑ Remains calm in high-pressure situations.
- ❑ Makes the most of limited resources.
- ❑ Demonstrates resilience in the face of setbacks.
- ❑ Understands change management.

Veterans Administration Competencies cont.

Creative Thinking

- ❑ Appreciates new ideas and approaches.
- ❑ Thinks and acts innovatively.
- ❑ Looks beyond current reality and the "status quo".
- ❑ Demonstrates willingness to take risks.
- ❑ Challenges assumptions.
- ❑ Solves problems creatively.
- ❑ Demonstrates resourcefulness.
- ❑ Fosters creative thinking in others.
- ❑ Allows and encourages employees to take risks.
- ❑ Identifies opportunities for new projects and acts on them.
- ❑ Rewards risk-taking and non-successes and values what was learned.

Systems Thinking

- ❑ Understands the complexities of the agency and how the "product" is delivered.
- ❑ Appreciates the consequences of specific actions on other parts of the system.
- ❑ Thinks in context.
- ❑ Knows how one's role relates to others in the organization.
- ❑ Demonstrates awareness of the purpose, process, procedures, and outcomes of one's work.
- ❑ Encourages and rewards collaboration.

Organizational Stewardship

- ❑ Demonstrates commitment to people.
- ❑ Empowers and trusts others.
- ❑ Develops leadership skills and opportunities throughout organization.
- ❑ Develops team-based improvement processes.
- ❑ Promotes future-oriented system change.
- ❑ Supports and encourages lifelong learning throughout the organization.
- ❑ Manages physical, fiscal, and human resources to increase the value of products and services.
- ❑ Builds links between individuals and groups in the organization.
- ❑ Integrates organization into the community.
- ❑ Accepts accountability for self, others, and the organization's development.
- ❑ Works to accomplish the organizational business plan.

Transportation Security Administration Core Competencies

The Transportation Security Administration (TSA) has posted its catalog of competencies containing both core and technical competencies at **www.tsa.gov/assets/pdf/competencies_and_definitions.pdf**. Below is a sampling of core competency definitions from the catalog.

Accountability	Holds self and others accountable for measurable high-quality, timely, and cost-effective results; determines objectives, sets priorities and delegates work; accepts responsibility for mistakes; complies with established control systems and rules.
Administration and Management	Applies business and management principles involved in strategic planning, resource allocation, and coordination of people and resources in support of organizational operations.
Administrative Procedures and Tasks	Performs administrative responsibilities following guidelines and procedures; provides guidance to others; coordinates services, researches problems, and recommends changes.
Arithmetic and Mathematical Reasoning	Performs computations such as addition, subtraction, multiplication, and division correctly; solves practical problems by choosing appropriately from a variety of mathematical techniques such as formulas and percentages.
Attention to Detail	Is thorough and precise when accomplishing a task with concern for all aspects of the job involved; double-checks the accuracy of information and work products to provide consistently accurate and high-quality work.
Coaching & Mentoring	Provides clear, behaviorally specific performance feedback; makes suggestions for improvement in a manner that builds confidence and preserves self-esteem; works with individuals to develop improvement plans and achieve performance goals.
Command Presence	Demonstrates confidence, credibility, and professionalism in presence, demeanor, and conduct in performance of duties within the work environment.
Conflict Management	Encourages creative tension and differences of opinions; anticipates and takes steps to prevent counter-productive confrontations; manages and resolves conflicts and disagreements in a constructive manner.
Conscientiousness	Demonstrates responsible and dependable behavior; takes responsibility for personal performance through a high level of effort and commitment.

Draft Qualification Standards

OPM is starting to draft Occupational Standards to include core competencies in the standard. View the drafts at **www.opm.gov/qualifications/Standards/DRAFTS/**. Below is the language from the Security Administration Series (0080) draft qualification standards. Currently, draft qualifiation standards may not be used to qualify applicants; however, these lists can provide a good source of keywords for your federal resume.

Accountability - Holds self and others accountable for measurable high-quality, timely, and cost-effective results. Determines objectives, sets priorities, and delegates work. Accepts responsibility for mistakes. Complies with established control systems and rules.

Attention to Detail - Is thorough when performing work and conscientious about attending to detail.

Customer Service - Works with clients and customers (that is, any individuals who use or receive the services or products that your work unit produces, including the general public, individuals who work in the agency, other agencies, or organizations outside the government) to assess their needs, provide information or assistance, resolve their problems, or satisfy their expectations; knows about available products and services; is committed to providing quality products and services.

Decision Making - Makes sound, well-informed, and objective decisions; perceives the impact and implications of decisions; commits to action, even in uncertain situations, to accomplish organizational goals; causes change.

Interpersonal Skills - Shows understanding, friendliness, courtesy, tact, empathy, concern, and politeness to others; develops and maintains effective relationships with others; may include effectively dealing with individuals who are difficult, hostile, or distressed; relates well to people from varied backgrounds and different situations; is sensitive to cultural diversity, race, gender, disabilities, and other individual differences.

Learning - Uses efficient learning techniques to acquire and apply new knowledge and skills; uses training, feedback, or other opportunities for self-learning and development.

Memory - Recalls information that has been presented previously.

Reading Comprehension - Understands and interprets written material, including technical material, rules, regulations, instructions, reports, charts, graphs, or tables; applies what is learned from written material to specific situations.

Self Management - Sets well-defined and realistic goals; displays a high level of initiative, effort, and commitment towards completing assignments in a timely manner; works with minimal supervision; is motivated to achieve; demonstrates responsible behavior.

Teamwork - Encourages and facilitates cooperation, pride, trust, and group identity; fosters commitment and team spirit; works with others to achieve goals.

Office of Personnel Management, Senior Executive Service, Executive Core Qualifications

Leading Change	Leading People	Results Driven	Business Acumen	Building Coalitions
Definitions				
This core qualification involves the ability to bring about strategic change, both within and outside the organization, to meet organizational goals. Inherent to this ECQ is the ability to establish an organizational vision and to implement it in a continuously changing environment.	This core qualification involves the ability to lead people toward meeting the organization's vision, mission, and goals. Inherent to this ECQ is the ability to provide an inclusive workplace that fosters the development of others, facilitates cooperation and teamwork, and supports constructive resolution of conflicts.	This core qualification involves the ability to meet organizational goals and customer expectations. Inherent to this ECQ is the ability to make decisions that produce high-quality results by applying technical knowledge, analyzing problems, and calculating risks.	This core qualification involves the ability to manage human, financial, and information resources strategically.	This core qualification involves the ability to build coalitions internally and with other federal agencies, state and local governments, nonprofit and private sector organizations, foreign governments, or international organizations to achieve common goals.
Competencies				
Creativity and Innovation External Awareness Flexibility Resilience Strategic Thinking Vision	Conflict Management Leveraging Diversity Developing Others Team Building	Accountability Customer Service Decisiveness Entrepreneurship Problem Solving Technical Credibility	Financial Management Human Capital Management Technology Management	Partnering Political Savvy Influencing/ Negotiating

Keywords and Phrases for Your Outline Format Federal Resume

You can find keywords for your federal resume from the vacancy announcements. Adding keywords is important for both a federal resume and a private industry resume. You can analyze the following sections: Duties, Specialized Experience, KSAs, and the Questionnaire. The ALL CAP WORDS in an Outline Format resume are phrases and keywords from the announcements. The human resources specialist and supervisor will recognize these skills from their announcement. Your goal is to match your resume as closely as possible to your target announcement and demonstrate that you DO have the experience for their position.

Where Do I Find Keywords?

- **Vacancy Announcements**: Focus your search in these sections: Duties, Specialized Experience, Qualifications, and the Assessment Questionnaire.

- **Agency or Organizational Mission**: You may find this in the vacancy announcement or on the agency's website.

- **Core Competencies**: See Step 4 for more information about core competencies.

- **Occupational Standards**: It's not widely known yet that occupational standards are superb sources for keywords to use in your resume!

How Do I Get Started?

Find two to five target vacancy announcements. Analyze the Duties, Qualifications, and Specialized Experience sections for keywords. Make a list of keywords and build your resume content using this first set of keywords. Once you have drafted a basic resume, you MUST MATCH this resume to specific job announcements by including keywords from that job announcement in your resume. Don't make the mistake so many applicants do and try to use the same resume to apply for a number of vacancy announcements. These applicants rarely get best qualified for a job.

Steps to Finding Keywords in a Vacancy Announcement

1. Save the vacancy announcement as an html file.

2. You will be reviewing these sections from the announcement for keywords:
    - ✪ Duties
    - ✪ Qualifications
    - ✪ Specialized Experience
    - ✪ Questionnaires
    - ✪ Agency or organization mission

3. Copy and paste these sections from the announcement into a word processing program such as Word or WordPerfect.

4. Enlarge the type to 14 or 16 points to make the print more readable.

5. Separate each sentence by increasing the line spacing for the entire document.

6. Delete useless words such as "the incumbent will" or "duties will encompass a variety of tasks including".

7. Underline or highlight keywords and skills that are significant to the position, such as "identifying deficiencies in human performance" and "recommending changes for correction."

How Many Keywords Do I Need?

At a minimum, include at least five to seven keywords in your resume. However, the more keywords you can include to help translate your experience into terms that the human resources specialist can clearly identify, the greater your chances of having the HR specialist understand how your qualifications match the desired qualifications in the vacancy announcement.

In the examples on the following pages, the found keywords are identified in bold type as well as listed at the end of each example.

Keywords can be found in the Duties and Qualifications sections of a vacancy announcement.

0132   Intelligence Specialist

DUTIES:
- **Conduct research for intelligence information** in preparation of routine studies.
- **Maintain database**(s) for the assigned function.
- **Analyze and evaluate information** to determine the reliability and credibility of the source and significance of the information.
- **Perform intelligence and information warfare C4I** system configuration control and requirements generation for the command.
- Recognize the role of **Naval Intelligence** in intelligence production and/or **collection management process**.

QUALIFICATIONS REQUIRED:

In order to qualify for this position, your resume must demonstrate at least one year of specialized experience at the GS/GG-07 grade level in the federal government (or in the private or public sector) performing some or all of the following duties: 1) utilizing intelligence techniques to provide **written products**, 2) **basic research** and **database management**, and 3) performing **intelligence and information warfare systems configuration control and requirements.**

KEYWORDS

- Conduct research for intelligence information
- Maintain databases
- Analyze and evaluate information for reliability and credibility
- Prepare intelligence and information warfare C4I
- Naval Intelligence and collection management process

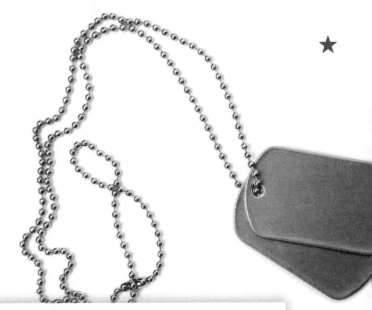

0301 Miscellaneous Administration and Program Series

DUTIES

In this position, you will provide **staff support** to the NPD Front Office to enhance the internal and external **efficiency and effectiveness** of the office. You will be responsible for independently **planning and carrying out assignments, resolving work problems**, interpreting policy, determining the approach to be taken and keeping the supervisor informed of progress. Typical work assignments include:

- Acts as **personal representative** of the NPD Assistant Administrator and Executive Officer in **telephonic and personal contacts** with high-ranking officials of FEMA and other departments and agencies, as well as executives of state and local governments and private industry.
- Researches assigned areas to provide supervisor with **authoritative information and material** which is utilized in preparation of **correspondence, reports, and policy documents** to facilitate meetings and negotiations.
- **Updates calendar** and prepares electronic briefing books for the NPD Assistant Administrator, including the upcoming daily, weekly and monthly calendar.
- **Schedules appointments and makes arrangements** for meetings and conferences upon request and direction of Executive Officer.
- **Ensures all travel policies** are followed to properly be reimbursed and authorizations/scheduling are executed for known events at least 10 business days in advance.

KEYWORDS

- Staff support and personal representative
- Customer support with high-ranking officials and executives
- Authoritative information and correspondence management
- Update calendar and manage electronic briefing books
- Schedule appointments and plan logistics
- Ensure complex travel plans

STEP 5

Keywords can be found in the OPM Classification Standards.

0341   Administrative Officer

CLASSIFICATION STANDARD

An administrative officer is a generalist. The total management process is his interest, and the proficiency required involves many aspects of management. **General management skills** are the paramount requirement. Though aspects such as **budget administration and personnel management** assume major importance in many positions and other aspects such as procurement and property management are also important in many jobs, no single functional, resource or service area forms a basis for the paramount skills.

Administrative officer positions typically include such duties and responsibilities as the following, or comparable duties:

1. Helping management to **identify its financial, personnel, and material needs and problems.**

2. **Developing budget estimates** and justifications; making sure that funds are used in accordance with the operating budget.

3. **Counseling management** in developing and maintaining sound organization structures, improving management methods and procedures, and seeing to the effective use of men, money, and materials.

4. **Collaborating** with personnel specialists in **finding solutions** to management problems arising out of changes in work which have an impact on jobs and employees.

5. **Advising on and negotiating contracts**, agreements, and cooperative arrangements with other government agencies, universities, or private organizations.

Administrative officer positions are mainly of two broad types. One type is the chief of a central administrative unit which provides services to a number of operating divisions, field offices, or other units each headed by an operating manager. The central administrative unit includes specialist positions in various areas such as **budget, data processing,** etc. The administrative unit chief has considerable authority to complete **personnel actions, obligate funds, make purchases,** etc.

KEYWORDS

- Management advisor
- Supervisor
- Budget advisor

- Problem-solving to management problems
- Advice on and negotiate contracts
- Data analyst

Keywords can be found in the KSAs and Quality Ranking Factors in Announcements.

0343   Management/ Program Analyst

DUTIES:

In this position, you will strengthen the Department's ability to perform homeland security functions by **developing policies,** conducting **special studies,** and providing **technical assistance.**   Typical work assignments include:

- **Developing and evaluating policies** in assigned program areas such as reviewing **existing strategic and workforce management plans** and proposing potential changes to ensure plans represent organizational priorities and ensuring that comprehensive succession management planning is in place.
- **Analyzing existing management techniques,** processes, and plans for improving organizational effectiveness.
- **Evaluating policies and recommending actions** to achieve organizational objectives such as analyzing organizational programs and processes to determine whether current procedures efficiently accomplish objectives and provide sufficient controls necessary for sound management.

Quality Ranking Factor: Applicants who possess the following experience may be rated higher than applicants who do not possess this experience. The desired experience for this position includes work in **strategic planning, succession management, workforce planning and data analysis of human resource information.** Management desires experience in applying **data analysis, metrics and performance measure analysis** to **workforce planning and the development,** execution and improvement of organizational effectiveness planning.

KEYWORDS

- Conduct special studies
- Technical assistance on projects
- Develop policies for strategic planning and workforce planning
- Data analysis and performance measure analysis
- Workforce planning and development

★

EXAMPLES OF KEYWORDS cont.

Keywords can be found in the Specialized Experience section.

1105 Purchasing Series

SPECIALIZED EXPERIENCE: At least one (1) year of specialized experience at the next lower grade (GS-05) or equivalent.

Specialized experience must include experience **drawing conclusions** and making routine recommendations by analyzing routine facts and conditions; **making comparison of prices**, discounts, delivery dates, or handling charges; **performing common arithmetic** practices used in business (e.g., discounts and warranties) sufficient to compare prices on recurring types of procurements, e.g., standard commercial items; **applying guideline** material by reading and interpreting procurement regulations and technical material; **translating the guidance into specific actions**, e.g., assisting in the preparation of solicitation documents; performing **writing techniques** to present factual information clearly and to **draft simple contract provisions** and supporting documentation; and/or dealing with others in a work relationship to present information orally and to accomplish a given purpose.

KEYWORDS

Procurement analyst; Procure products and services for internal customers; Research comparison prices, discounts and delivery dates; Apply guidelines and interpret procurement regulations and technical materials; Assist in preparation of solicitation documents; Draft simple contract provisions; Collaborate with others and brief supervisors

Keywords can be found in mission statements.

1152 Production Control

MISSION STATEMENT:
This position is a Production Specialist located in the **Operations** Department Scheduling Branch of Portsmouth Naval Shipyard. The individual selected assists the **Scheduling** Division Head in developing management strategies for all **nuclear and non-nuclear work** on all availabilities assigned to the Shipyard, all off-yard Selected Restricted Availabilities, Technical Availabilities, etc. and Shipyard Other Productive Work (OPW) projects.

DUTIES

Serve as an **assistant system manager** for the **development**, **implementation**, and **operation** of the **mainframe computer scheduling system** as well as **local application scheduling systems. Configure personal computer workstations** including installation of operating systems, application software, and updates for scheduler use. Prepare nuclear and non-nuclear work and test schedules for nuclear submarines, non-nuclear surface ships and service craft. Provide automation support to **maintain accurate databases**.

KEYWORDS

Analyze and evaluate production control schedule; Review production specifications and ensure equipment readiness; Implement operations for computer scheduling systems; Configure and update personal computer workstations; Prepare nuclear and non-nuclear work and test schedules; Maintain databases

STEP 5

Keywords can be found in the Questionnaires.

General Supply Specialist, GS-2001

For each task in the following group, choose the statement from the list below that best describes your experience and/or training. Darken the oval corresponding to that statement in Section 25 of the Qualifications and Availability Form C. Please select only one letter for each item.

- A- I have not had education, training or experience in performing this task.
- B- I have had education or training in performing the task, but have not yet performed it on the job.
- C- I have performed this task on the job. My work on this task was monitored closely by a supervisor or senior employee to ensure compliance with proper procedures.
- D- I have performed this task as a regular part of a job. I have performed it independently and normally without review by a supervisor or senior employee.
- E- I am considered an expert in performing this task. I have supervised performance of this task or am normally the person who is consulted by other workers to assist them in doing this task because of my expertise.

4. **Interpret supply management regulations**, laws, concepts, principles to determine inventory management requirements.

5. **Use automated systems** to maintain records of supply items in inventory.

6. **Establish and implement policies**, procedural guidance and instruction for personal property control.

7. Recommend and **implement supply management policies** and procedures to **ensure operational accountability of property**.

KEYWORDS

- Interpret supply management regulations
- Utilize supply automated systems
- Implement personal property control policies
- Ensure operational accountability of property
- Provide customer services

STEP 6

★ **Write Your Outline Format and Paper Federal Resume**

Many applicants consider this step to be the most difficult.

...which is why we want to introduce to you the Outline Format federal resume with keywords.

The Outline Format is highly regarded by human resources specialists for being very easy to read. The pertinent information that the HR specialist is looking for stands out much better in an Outline Format resume. Here are some of the key features:

- Small paragraphs are used for readability.
- ALL CAPS keywords match keywords in the announcement.
- Accomplishments are included in the resume.
- This format copies and pastes quickly and easily into USAJOBS.

Federal resumes are different from private industry resumes for a number of reasons. Here is a quick list of differences to keep in mind when you are converting your private industry resume into a federal resume.

Private Industry and TAP Resume	Federal Resume
Typically 1-2 pages	3-5 pages based on specific character lengths (use full character lengths if possible)
Creative use of bold, underline, and other graphics	Text file, chronological, traditional format with no graphics; use CAPS for enhancement in lieu of graphics
No federal elements required (i.e., SSN, supervisor's name and phone, salary, veterans' preference, etc.)	Federal elements required (SSN, supervisor's name and phone, salary, veterans' preference, etc.)
Short accomplishment bullets focused on results	Accomplishment bullets focused on the details of "how" you attained results
Branded "headline"	Focus on the KSAs and competencies required in the announcement.
Keywords are important	Keywords are imperative
Focus on accomplishments; less details for position descriptions	Use blend of accomplishments and duties description with details
Profit motivated, product oriented, select customer base	Fiscal responsibility and grants, budgets, cost control, implementation of programs, legislation, serving the American public

Additional Special Considerations for Military

Military	Federal Resume
List dates of Reserve service and active duty service	Include approx. average hours for Reserve service, i.e., 20 years of Reserve service with deployments, equals six years of full-time work at 52 weeks per year
Include applicable awards and indicate justification for attaining award	List most awards and honors and include justification
Translate military acronyms and jargon	Translate most military acronyms and jargon, but use acronyms if the vacancy announcement uses the acronyms (i.e., DOD, DON, USMC, etc.)
Quantify and qualify military activities or acronyms	Quantify and qualify military activities or acronyms
Only include military schools/education related to the announcement	Include military service schools; indicate resident classes and total hours

The private industry resume is generally two pages long and is too short to be an effective federal resume.

Alex Peterson

600 Orkney Street
Baltimore, MD 21211
(555) 555-5555
alex.peterson@email.com

JOB VACANCY SPECIFICS

- Job Announcement Number: XXX
- Job Title: XXXX
- Series & Grade: XXXX

PERSONAL INFORMATION

- Social Security Number: XXX-XX-XXXX
- Country of Citizenship: U.S.A
- Veterans' Preference: VEOA, Eligible Veteran

WORK EXPERIENCE

Maryland Air National Guard,

Cyber Transport Apprentice, Martin State Airport, MD, November 2009 to Present

- Install and configure REDCOMM basic access module telephone switching networks that connect 48 telephone lines.
- Fabricate, terminate and inter connect wiring for LAN (Local Area Network) systems.
- Trouble shoot and repair LANs.
- Supervisor: TSgt Bernie Milton, (555) 555-5555. Supervisor may be contacted.
- Hours Per Month: 16   Pay Grade: E-5

United States Navy

Operations Specialist, Norfolk, VA, July 2005 to May 2008

- Operated navigational radar to determine movement of objects detected by radar for the purpose of bearing, range and speed.
- Disseminated radar contact information over internal communication network to maintain the safety and security of the ship.
- Completed over 150 damage control maintenance checks with zero discrepancies which resulted in the ship's readiness for deployment.
- Supervisor: Chief Tony Clark, (555) 555-5555. Supervisor may be contacted.
- Hours Per Week: 40   Pay Grade: E-5

Office Assistant, Navy Amphibious Base, Little Creek, VA November 2003 to June 2005

- Performed data entry.
- Maintained personnel records.
- Maintained routing and tracking of paper work.
- Supervisor: Lieutenant Rossman. Supervisor is no longer at this command.
- Hours Per Week: 40   Pay Grade: E-3

STEP 6

General Nutrition Center, Baltimore, MD, September 1998 to May 2003

Retail Salesman

• Worked with customers to determine nutritional needs.
• Performed purchasing, shipping, receiving, and accounts payable.
• Increased sales by 15%, by providing focused and individualized customer service.
• Supervisor: Buddy Donaldson, (555) 555-5555. Supervisor may be contacted.
• Hours Per Week: 15-20 Hourly Rate: $12.50

TICC, The Internet Connectivity Company, Baltimore, MD, May 1995 to September 1998

Customer Support Representative

• Assisted customers with internet connectivity using dedicated T-1 access lines to connect to TICC.
• Responded to customer questions about internet connectivity through email.
• Provided in house training to new employees.
• Supervisor: Ted Brighton. TICC is no longer in business.
• Hours Per Week: 20   Hourly Rate: $9.50

EDUCATION

University of Maryland, College Park, MD, September 2000 to May 2001

Successfully completed 15 credit hours towards a Bachelor's Degree in Computer Science.

Community College Baltimore County (CCBC), Catonsville, MD, September 1993 to May 2000

Associate's Degree in Computer Science

Rockville High School, Rockville, MD, September 1984 to May 1987

High School Diploma

QUALIFICATIONS

Training

• Cyber Transport Apprentice Course (680 Hours), Keesler AFB, MS, September 2010
• Information Fundamentals Basic Course (328 Hours), Joint Base Andrews, MD, April 2010
• Search and Rescue School (40 Hours), Afloat Training Group, Norfolk, VA, March 2006
• Tactical Decision Support Subsystem School (40 Hours), Navy Base, Point Loma, CA, October 2005
• Operations Specialist "A" School (360 Hours), Navy Base, Dam Neck, VA, September 2005
• Roll-on Roll-off Discharge School (80 Hours), Naval Amphibious Base, Coronado CA, December 2003
• Seamanship Apprentice School (80 Hours), Recruit Training Command, Great Lakes IL, October 2003
• Recruit Training (157 Hours), Recruit Training Command, Great Lakes, IL, September 2003

Skills

• Microsoft Office Suite; Word, Excel, PowerPoint
• C Programming

Certifications

• CompTIA Security+ Certification, October 2010

The new federal resume was written in the Outline Format and entered into the USAJOBS resume builder.

ALEX PETERSON
600 Orkney Street
Baltimore, MD 21211
(444) 444-4444
Alex.peterson@email.com

Availability: **Job Type:** Permanent, Temporary, Term, Internships, Telework
Work Schedule: Full-Time, Job Sharing

Desired locations: United States - AL - Adamsville
United States - AL - Adger
United States - AL - Addison
United States - AL - Acmar
United States - AL - Abernant
United States - AL - Abbeville
Bahrain
United States - CA
United States - DC

Work Experience: **Maryland Air National Guard (MDNG)**   **11/2009 - Present**
175th Communications Squadron, 175th Wing   **Salary:** 2,800.00 USD Per Month
Martin State Airport   **Hours per week:** 40
Baltimore, MD   United States
CYBER TRANSPORT STAFF SERGEANT
Supervisor: TSgt Bernie Milton (5555555555)
Okay to contact this Supervisor: Yes
Active U.S. Military Secret Clearance

SECRET CLEARANCE.
RECRUITED BY MDNG for my DEMONSTRATED SUPERIOR KNOWLEDGE OF IT OPERATING SYSTEMS, applications, ADP equipment configurations and interconnecting components, my proven customer service record, and my problem-solving and communication skills.

CYBER TRANSPORT IT SPECIALIST currently serving in MDNG. As a NETWORK TECHNICIAN for the 175th Communications Squadron and the 175th Wing, provide essential IT customer support services for up to 500 staff.

COMPUTER NETWORK HARDWARE AND COMMUNICATION EQUIPMENT SPECIALIST: Deploy, sustain, troubleshoot, and repair standard voice, data, and video network infrastructure systems, IP detection systems and cryptographic equipment. Perform, coordinate, integrate, and supervise network design, configuration, operation, defense, restoration, and improvements. Analyze capabilities and performance, identify problems, and take corrective action. Fabricate, terminate, and interconnect wiring and associated network infrastructure devices. Apply knowledge obtained from reading and understanding highly technical manuals. Apply extensive knowledge of IT operating systems, applications, and ADP equipment configurations and components.

ESTABLISH AND MANAGE INTERNET GATEWAY COMMUNICATIONS secure IP and voice service (VoIP) within 30 minutes using Theater Deployable Communication (TDC) Integrated Communication Access Package (ICAP). Provide EFFECTIVE, HIGH QUALITY IT CUSTOMER SERVICE and support, including in remote locations, by ensuring reliable customer access to secure and non-secure networks for up to 100 users.
• Set up and configure REDCOM Basic Access Module telephone switching networks.
• Fabricate and connect category 5 and fiber optic network cables.
• Troubleshoot to diagnose and repair computer network hardware and software problems.
• Install software updates and patches on existing network infrastructure.
• Work closely with supervisor to maintain network security.

USN, USS Stout
Norfolk, VA   United States
OPERATIONS SPECIALIST, E-5
Supervisor: Chief Tony Clark (5555555555)
Okay to contact this Supervisor: Yes

07/2005 - 04/2008
Hours per week: 40

MONITORED AND EVALUATED STRATEGIC INFORMATION in ship's Combat Information Center (CIC), and made recommendations to command and control regarding tactical procedures. Tracked and identified up to 40 friend-or-foe vessels at a time for ship commander and up to 30 CIC staff. Applied extensive knowledge of IT operating systems, applications, and ADP equipment configurations and components.

COMPLETED OVER 150 COMPUTER HARDWARE and electronic diagnostic checks with zero discrepancies resulting in ship's readiness for deployment. Performed all basic electric maintenance in the CIC. Applied knowledge obtained from reading and understanding highly technical manuals.

COORDINATED AND USED SECURE AND NON-SECURE NETWORKING EQUIPMENT during over 30 training exercises with air, sea, and land units, including live-fire exercises and Naval Battle Group exercises.

MANAGED AND MAINTAINED WORK CENTER COMPUTER and highly controlled technical publications (manuals) inventory.

PLAYED A KEY ROLE IN SHIP'S DISASTER RECOVERY TEAM. Trained to switch to redundant backup systems without loss of command and control in the event of catastrophic equipment failure. Supervised five more junior communications staff.

PARTICIPATED IN MARITIME PROTECTION/FORCE INTERDICTION OPERATIONS in Iraqi territorial waters (North Persian Gulf) claimed by Iran and designed to protected Iraqi oil platforms from Iranian military incursions, February-March 2008.
• Granted special shore leave liberty as reward for exceptional performance by the Captain of the Stout.

USN, Navy Amphibious Base
Little Creek, VA   United States
OFFICE ASSISTANT, E-3
Supervisor: Lieutenant Rossman (7033333333)
Okay to contact this Supervisor: Yes

11/2003 - 06/2005
Hours per week: 49

PERFORMED DATA ENTRY, maintained 250 personnel records, and controlled routing and tracking of paperwork. Performed administrative and clerical work. Received visitors, answered telephone calls and sorted incoming mail. Organized files and operated modern office equipment such as word processing computers and copying machines.
• Performed office personnel administration;
• Maintained records and official publications;
• Served as office manager.

OPERATION IRAQI FREEDOM PARTICIPANT, 01/2004-03/2005: Based in Kuwait, trained to go to Iraq as a ship-to-shore logistics Seaman in support of US Marine combat operations.

CHOSEN FOR TSUNAMI RELIEF TEAM, 12/2004: Chosen for stand-by team after Indian Ocean Tsunami, and rapidly deployed to Southeast Asia for tsunami relief. Conducted essential relief operations for 3 months in tsunami-affected areas in Thailand, Sri Lanka, and the Maldives under harsh conditions.

Education:

Community College of Baltimore County Catonsville, MD United States
Associate's Degree 06/2000

Major: Information Technology

University of Maryland College Park, MD United States
Some College Coursework Completed

Credits Earned: 32 Semester hours
Major: Computer Science
Relevant Coursework, Licenses and Certifications:
Computer Science

Job Related Training:

CERTIFICATIONS
• CompTIA Security+ Certification, Keesler AFB, MS (October 2010)
• Air Force Trainer Certification, Joint Base Andrews, MD (December 2010)
• Active U.S. Military Secret Clearance

TRAINING
• Air Force Security and Cyber Transport Certification Apprenticeship Course (October 2010)
• Cyber Transport Apprentice Course (680 Hours), Joint Base Andrews, MD (September 2010)
• Information Fundamentals Basic Course (328 Hours), Keesler AFB, MS (April 2010)
• Search and Rescue School (40 Hours), Afloat Training Group, Norfolk , VA (March 2006)
• Tactical Decision Support Subsystem School (40 Hours), Navy Base, Point Loma, CA (October 2005)
• Operations Specialist "A" School (360 Hours), Navy Base, Dam Neck, VA (September 2005)
• Roll-on Roll-off Discharge School (80 Hours), Naval Amphibious Base, Coronado, CA, (December 2003)
• Seamanship Apprentice School (80 Hours), Recruit Training Command, Great Lakes, IL (October 2003)
• Recruit Training (157 Hours), Recruit Training Command, Great Lakes, IL (September 2003)

Additional Information:

SUMMARY OF TECHNOLOGY SKILLS

Applications: MS Office Professional 2010, Filemaker Pro Database, MS Visual C++ 6.0, MS Visual Basic 6.0, Norton Ghost, Symantec Antivirus, MacAfee Total Protection, Partition Magic

Operating Systems: Microsoft Server 2003, Microsoft Window NT 4.0, Workstation and Server, Microsoft Windows 95, 98, XP, Vista and Windows 7, Cisco Router/Switches IOS, MS-DOS, Digital VMS for VAX, UNIX

Hardware: Intel and AMD Based Computers, Cisco 2621, 2811 Routers, Cisco 900, 2950, 2960, 3550, 3560 Switches, Promina 400 Multiplexer, VPN Concentrator 3000 Series, Taclane-Micro Encryption Device, KG-84 Encryption Device, REDCOM Basic Access Module, RAID 0-6, PDP-11 Minicomputer

Protocols: TCP/IP, BGP, OSPF, EIGRP, IGRP, RIPv2, IS-IS, DHCP, DNS, RTP, UDP, RAS, IPv4, IPv6

Programming Languages: C, MASM, Pascal, Visual Basic, MUMPS

Networking: Ethernet, WLANs, LANs

STEP 6

PROFESSIONAL PROFILE

• Highly experienced, dedicated, and professional Information Technology (IT) Customer Support Specialist, with over five years of providing effective, high quality IT customer support services to diverse user communities, including in remote locations and under adverse conditions.

• Extensive Air National Guard experience and training in customer support, computer networking, repair and telecommunications. Highly relevant Naval experience in the Combat Information Center of a modern US warship relevant to working in a fast-paced, problem solving environment.

• Excellent and proven Attention To Detail, Problem Solving, Oral Communication, and Customer Service skills and abilities.

• Superior broad and deep knowledge of operating systems/applications, knowledge of ADP equipment configurations and interconnecting components, and the ability to read and understand technical manuals.

• Decorated Operation Iraqi Freedom veteran. CompTIA Security+ Certification.

AWARDS AND HONORS

Navy "E" Ribbon
Good Conduct Medal
Navy Expeditionary Medal
National Defense Service Medal
Global War On Terrorism Expeditionary Medal
Global War On Terrorism Service Medal
Humanitarian Service Medal
Air Force Longevity Medal
Sea Service Deployment Ribbon

OBJECTIVES/GOALS:
- General Administrative, Clerical and Office Services– 0300/0399-GS-07
- Public Affairs Specialist (0135), GS 07/09

Eligible for Noncompetitive Appointment of Certain Military Spouses – PCS Orders Attached

Natalie Richardson

Address
Fort Lee, VA 23801
(912) 444-4444
email

MARKETING AND ADVERTISING QUALIFICATIONS

- Marketing research, strategic planning, customer service and sales talents nurtured by in depth and diverse advertising, and administrative experience.
- Knowledge of International Business approaches and cultural sensitivities gained by living abroad.
- Complete corporate branding systems including logos: pictorial, letterform, combination image and text.
- French fluency and adequate Spanish capabilities.

MARKETING, ADVERTISING, AND SALES EXPERIENCE

Twelve years of customer service experience.   Excellent verbal, written communications and interpersonal skills developed through being self-employed.

Will motivate those around me. Excellent work ethic and strong leadership.

Exceptional ability to relate to people at any level of business and management as well as culture because of extensive international travel having lived abroad in various circumstances.

PROFESSIONAL EXPERIENCE

Base Coupon Connection *Fort Stewart, Georgia   Sept. 2010- Feb.. -2011 (Owner)*
OFFERS FROM LOCAL BUSINESSES SERVING THE MILITARY AND THEIR FAMILIES
Business Card Wholesalers *Conyers, Georgia 2005-2009 (Owner)*

Multi-Care Health & Rehab, LLC *Conyers, Georgia 2004 (Public Relations)*

Phoebe's Boutique *Lithonia, Georgia 2002-2004 (General Manager / Personal Assistant)*

EDUCATION

DeKalb Technical Institute, (Covington, Georgia)
National Emergency Medical Technician Intermediate December 2000
Yamoussoukro International School (Cote d'Ivoire, West Africa)
High School Diploma Sept 96 – May 99

1

These networking and private industry resumes will not work well for federal job applications.

Natalie Richardson

Address
Fort Lee, VA 23801
(912) 444-4444

WORK EXPERIENCE:

Base Coupon Connection *Fort Stewart, Georgia   Sept. 2010- Feb.. -2011 (Owner)*
OFFERS FROM LOCAL BUSINESSES SERVING THE MILITARY AND THEIR FAMILIES

- Owned and operated BaseCouponConnection.com
- Sold 3, 6, and 12 month contracts to local businesses.
- Responsible for marketing local businesses to military members in Iraq with free shipping, phone messages, and free personal delivery on gifts for their loved ones. (Send It To Your Sweetie)
- Maintained categories for Fort Stewart, GA and Fort Gordon, GA: with sub-categories which included Restaurant guide/reviews, Send It To Your Sweetie and Game Source Forum (for Deployed service members), Coupons, Deals, Freebies and Map It.
- Free for the military and their families to access and use all offers provided from participating local businesses.
- Designed website and all aspects of Advertising/Marketing.

Business Card Wholesalers *Conyers, Georgia 2005-2009 (Owner)*   Owned and operated Business Card Wholesalers.

- Sold thousands of printing products to small businesses on a daily basis.
- Designed and distributed orders within seven days of every order.
- Conducted all aspects of accounting.
- Maintained customer relations by calling, dropping by and making re-orders within 6 months of previous orders.
- Photographed clients and worked with customers to achieve their desired customized product.
- Currently accepting re-orders and working with customers long-distance.

EDUCATION:

National Emergency Medical Technician Intermediate
DeKalb Technical Institute, Covington, GA 30014
GPA: 4.0 of a maximum 4.0, 1 year course.
Certification November 7, 2001

Outline Format federal resume in the USAJOBS Resume Builder. Features keywords, phrases and accomplishments.

NATALIE RICHARDSON
Address
Ft. Lee, VA 23801
Day Phone: (912) 444-4444
Email: Natalie@email.com

Work Experience: **BaseCouponConnection.com**   **09/2010 - 02/2011**
Fort Stewart, GA   United States   **Salary:** 2,160.00 USD Per Hour
                                                       Hours per week: 70

PARTNER/MANAGER
Supervisor: Natalie Richardson(self) (912) 444-4444
Okay to contact this Supervisor: Yes
MARKETING PROGRAM FOR MILITARY FAMILIES WITH FAMILY MEMBER IN IRAQ.
Developed, owned, managed and operated business that sold marketing contracts to local businesses. Marketed "Send It To Your Sweetie" program targeting free services to military families with members in Iraq for shipping, phone messages, and personal delivery of gifts for their loved ones. Met with base command to ensure all regulations and policies were met.

• Accomplishment: Conceptualized a successful program for family members to send gifts and messages to military personnel. More than 2,500 messages were sent through this program in just six months. Sold business in less than 6 months for a substantial profit.

COMMUNICATIONS. Wrote business plan and developed all aspects of advertising and marketing. Performed cold calls on business customers and followed up with written proposals. Created and delivered PowerPoint presentations to groups of various sizes. Organized and prepared mailings to families and businesses.

WEBSITE DESIGN: Designed website and prepared spreadsheet to track monthly views and clicks. Due to volume of business, interviewed and hired 3 contractors to assist with billing, designing ads, and updating website.

Business Card Wholesalers   **06/2005 - 06/2009**
Conyers, GA   United States   **Salary:** 3,000.00 USD Per Month
                                             Hours per week: 75

MANAGER
Supervisor: Steven Jones, Phone: (555) 555-5555
Okay to contact this Supervisor: Yes
CREATIVE PRODUCTION: Sold and created full-color, personalized business cards to small businesses. Planned and organized work; efficiently and effectively processed the sale, design, ordering and delivery of product. Ensured quality control, and timeliness for re-orders.

• Established a successful in-home business with local producers of business cards. Contracted with more than 15 vendors and tracked orders for more than 200 customers in two years. Efficiently set up and managed own schedule and schedule for automatic reordering.

CUSTOMER SERVICES: Provided administrative support to customers and vendors. Prepared and sent invoices, collected balances due. Conducted all aspects of accounting.

COMMUNICATION: Corresponded with clients by email and phone, ensured correct grammar, spelling and format. Made cold calls on small businesses – utilized interpersonal skills to develop customer base of 300 businesses within 6 months.

COMPUTER SKILLS: : Utilized typing speed of 45 wpm, Microsoft Suite programs for reports and communication, as well as Photoshop, Illustrator and Corel software to design cards.

Demonstrated strong customer services skills; multi-tasked and worked under pressure and constant deadlines. Maintained customer relations; photographed clients and worked with customers to achieve their desired customized product.

Multi-Care Health and Rehab LLC
Conyers, GA   United States

02/2004 - 01/2005
Salary: 2,300.00 USD Per Hour
Hours per week: 40

PUBLIC RELATIONS
Supervisor: Gina Johnson (777) 777-7777
Okay to contact this Supervisor: Yes
BUSINESS DEVELOPMENT AND COMMUNICATIONS: Represented chiropractic clinic public relations, made new business contacts, mended old contacts. Developed lasting business relationships with store managers, district managers and their assistants both inside and outside the office. Scheduled health screenings involving blood pressure, glucose and cholesterol testing. Ensured excellent service. Successfully increased patient roster by an average of 5 new patients per week.

Phoebe's Boutique
Lithonia, GA   United States

04/2002 - 02/2004
Salary: 2,580.00 USD Per Year
Hours per week: 40

MANAGER
Supervisor: Marcia Lopez (999) 999-9999
Okay to contact this Supervisor: Yes
ADMINISTRATION: Performed office and store administration including management of files and official records, training, payroll and reporting. Communicated effectively orally and in writing. Developed, wrote, standardized and regulated customer service procedures, policies and systems.

COMMUNICATIONS: Communicated with diverse customers, vendors, management to increase sales and resolve problems. Greeted and assisted customers with special requests. Trained staff to deliver excellent customer service.

COMPUTER SKILLS: Utilized computer skills to design website and regulate maintenance for user effectiveness. Used Microsoft Word for correspondence and Excel for reports. Ensured accuracy, correct grammar, spelling, punctuation and syntax.

MANAGED STAFF AND BUDGET: Planned and organized work for sales staff; managed budgeting for cost effective sales planning, directed all tasks and aspects of controlling, maintaining and rotating inventory. Designed store layout and product presentations.

MARKETING SOLUTIONS: Gathered pertinent data, and recognized solutions to initiate and conduct successful storewide marketing campaigns. Controlled and minimized expenses to maximize profit through selected business improvements.

Education:	**DeKalb Technical Institute** Covington, GA United States Professional 11/2001 **GPA:** 4.0 of a maximum 4.0 **Major:** Emergency Medical Technician Intermediate
Job Related Training:	CERTIFICATION: National Emergency Medical Technician Intermediate, Certification November 7, 2001 TRAINING: 2004, Two Day Public Relations Training Seminar, David Singer Enterprises, Inc., Clearwater, FL 33755 Individual Coaching, Teleconference Training, Public Speaking, Insurance Billing & Coding, Staff Training, How to Book and Deliver Outside Lectures, and Patient Policies. Print Production, Corporate Branding, Visual Layout and Composition, Print Imaging and Design, Expressive Drawing, Muralist, Photography.

Language Skills:

Language	Spoken	Written	Read
French	Advanced	Intermediate	None

STEP 6

Additional Information:

SUMMARY OF QUALIFICATIONS
• More than 12 years' experience in customer service, sales, and business administration.
• Demonstrated ability to plan and implement administrative improvements.
• Outstanding oral and written communication skills, coupled with organizational expertise and attention to detail.
• Strong interpersonal skills; knowledge of and sensitivity to diverse cultures gained by living abroad. Exceptional ability to relate to groups and individuals at all levels of business and management in structured and unstructured situations.
• Dynamic skills in marketing research, data gathering and strategic planning, analysis, developing and leading complex projects. Skilled in corporate branding systems including logos: pictorial, letterform, combination image and text.
• Problem solver; highly organized, and able to prioritize and meet multiple deadlines.
• Working knowledge of effective group relationships; able to lead, motivate and train staff and build consensus with all stakeholders.
• Demonstrated ability to make solid decisions with highest level of integrity.
• Highly proficient in Microsoft Suite and Corel.
• Type 45 wpm with 3 errors or less.
• Personal strengths: Ability to attain and exceed goals, strong work ethic, attentive to detail, competent, professional, and positive.

Thanks to your awesome resume skills, I have landed a job! It is a GS-9 position as a public affairs specialist. I will be in charge of all the advertising for the recruiting battalion here in VA.

I LOVE YOU GUYS!
(They hired me based on my resume and questionnaire - they didn't even ask for an interview!)

-- Natalie

What makes a resume "federal" are the following "compliance details" that must be included in your federal resume. Be sure to include the following sections / information in your resume:

Job Information

Announcement number, title, and grade.

Personal Information

Full name, mailing address (with ZIP code), day and evening phone numbers (with area code), Social Security number, country of citizenship, veterans' preference, reinstatement eligibility, and highest federal civilian grade held. Social Security number is required in Application Manager but not in USAJOBS.

Education

Colleges or universities, name, city, and state, majors and type and year of any degrees received (if no degree, show total credits earned and indicate whether semester or quarter hours). High school name, city, and state. (Some announcements do not ask for high school.)

Work Experience

Job title, duties, and accomplishments, employer's name and address, supervisor's name and phone number, starting and ending dates (month and year), hours per week, salary, and indicate whether or not your current supervisor may be contacted. Prepare a separate entry for each job.

Other Qualifications

Job-related training courses (title and year), job-related skills, job-related certificates and licenses, job-related honors, awards, and special accomplishments.

To get your first federal resume draft written:

- Start writing your first draft using the Classification Standards.

- Then, later you can tailor this draft to specific vacancy announcements.

Links to the Classification Standards:

White Collar Positions: www.opm.gov/fedclass/html/gsseries.asp

Trades, Craft, and Labor Positions: www.opm.gov/fedclass/html/fwsdocs.asp

---

STEP 6

Inventory Management Series, GS 2010

Inventory Management Series, GS-2010   TS-117 July 1992

The three primary functions that characterize the occupation are management, coordination, and control of inventory and systems of inventory management.

1. Inventory Management includes the integrated management and control of assigned items of material. The work involves a number of processes such as:

  (a) Requirements Determination - Planning for and determining current and future supply requirements to meet customer needs;

  (b) Material Distribution - Planning and determining the distribution and positioning of supplies among major supply stations, stock points, or using activities;

  (c) Procurement Authorization - Preparing recommendations and directives for the procurement of material, indicating the types of items, quantities, and at all times, the sources; and

  (d) Funds Management - Analyzing planned or scheduled material requirements and forecasts to determine categories and quantities of items, as well as funds required.

Quality Assurance Series, GS 1910

Knowledge and Skill Required

Quality assurance work in general requires application of the following kinds of knowledge and skills:

-   Knowledge of quality assurance/control methods, principles, and practices, including statistical analysis and sampling techniques;

-   Knowledge of pertinent product characteristics and applicable production maintenance, or repair methods and processes;

-   Knowledge of inspection, test, and measurement techniques;

-   Knowledge of the relationship of quality assurance to other activities such as contract administration, engineering, supply;

-   Skill in interpreting and applying product specifications, technical data, regulations, policy statements, and other guideline materials;

-   Skill in conducting studies and investigations, problem analysis, and developing logical and documented recommendations;

★ FACTOR EVALUATION SYSTEM (FES)

STEP 6

The Factor Evaluation System (FES) is part of the Classification Standards and includes nine factors that are part of most nonsupervisory GS positions. These descriptions are used for assigning grades under the GS system and are highly useful for improving your resume.

Look through the FES definitions in the Classification Standard for your target position. Where applicable, add the answers to the following key FES questions into your resume to dramatically improve your federal resume content.

KNOWLEDGE

- What knowledge do you have to help you do your job?

SUPERVISORY CONTROLS

- What kind of supervisory control do you have?
- Or do you work independently?

GUIDELINES USED

- What guidelines do you use to do your job?
- What laws, regulations or references?
- List all legislation, manuals, SOPs, policies, references

COMPLEXITY

- What is the scope of your position?

SCOPE & EFFECT

- Who do you talk to and work with?
- What is the scope of your work?
- Is it local, regional, worldwide?

PERSONAL CONTACTS AND PURPOSE OF CONTACTS

- Who are your customers?
- Are they nearby or do you work with them through email, etc.?
- How many customers do you support?

Before Resume: WITHOUT THE FES INFORMATION

Administrative Assistant (40 hrs per wk) (Massachusetts Air National Guard) Jan 08 – Present. Provide administrative support to the Chief of Staff (Massachusetts Air National Guard). Provide reports to queries on personnel matters utilizing data systems RCAS and IPERMS. Track suspense's, Executive Summaries, correspondence, briefings, and investigations utilizing an electronic log system. Review Executive Summaries for content, format, and administrative errors. Maintain Payroll Worksheets for 35 personnel monitoring hours worked and vacations taken, and provide summary reports to supervisors and finance personnel. Manage Moral and Welfare fund requests for Massachusetts National Guard units by reviewing requests for legality, administrative correctness, submitting the paperwork to the State Military Department, and coordinating issuance of checks. Monitor the Chief of Staff's calendar for appointments and events. Assist in developing/mentoring new personnel both enlisted and officer with office procedures.

After Resume: WITH THE FES INFORMATION

ADMINISTRATIVE ASSISTANT (40 hrs per wk) (Mass. Air National Guard)
Assistant to the Chief of Staff who oversees 3,000 Mass. National Guard Soldiers. Work independently to support all administrative, personnel, correspondence and payroll administration for the director.

COMPLEX ADMINISTRATION: Highly skilled in supporting multiple battalion deployments and re-integration and readiness during and following the ending of Iraq and Afghanistan. ACCOMPLISHMENT: Improved support for deployed and emergency support for the guardsmen. Organized and coordinated efficient ceremonies and events. Managed paperwork for complex deployments.

IMPLEMENT THE NATIONAL GUARD TECHNICIAN HANDBOOK. Implement and administer "The Technician Act of 1968", Public Law 90-486, for all support services for Reserves and Active duty personnel.

REPORTS AND DATABASE ADMINISTRATION AND COMPUTER SKILLS. Produce reports to queries on personnel matters utilizing data systems RCAS and IPERMS. Track suspenses, Executive Summaries, correspondence, briefings, and investigations utilizing an electronic log system.

CUSTOMER SERVICES FOR THE GUARD PERSONNEL: Manage Moral and Welfare fund requests for Massachusetts National Guard units by reviewing requests for legality and administrative correctness, submitting the paperwork to the State Military Department, and coordinating issuance of checks.

★ CHECKLIST FOR COMPLETING YOUR ONLINE RESUME

❑ Provide ALL the information requested including documentation required for the position.

❑ Answer ALL job-related questions to the best of your ability. Include accurate details of your experience, education, or training in the narrative input fields provided.

❑ Use ALL portions of the application to provide unique and exemplary information that sets you apart from other candidates.

❑ Present your most important job-related competencies and accomplishments.

❑ Read the vacancy announcement carefully from top to bottom.

❑ Stress actions and achievements.

❑ Present information in a polished (and accurate!) manner.

❑ Count your characters in your job blocks:
- USAJOBS has 5,000 character limit per job.
- AvueCentral has 4,000 character limit per job.

SELL YOURSELF!

DO!

Collect Information

- ❏ Locate all of your written career papers, such as resumes, evaluations, and position descriptions.
- ❏ Find your list of training classes.
- ❏ Find or order your college transcripts.
- ❏ Find your DD-214 and other veteran's documents.

Research Announcements

- ❏ Find at least one announcement that is correct for you.
- ❏ Analyze the keywords from duties, qualifications, and questions.
- ❏ Analyze the one year specialized experience that is important for your announcement.

Federal Resume Writing

- ❏ Make a list of accomplishments from your last two positions.
- ❏ Be sure to mention the types of customers you serve, and list the customers if you can.
- ❏ Write your first federal resume that will focus your resume toward one position.
- ❏ After you write ONE resume and target this toward ONE job series, you can write another resume version – with additional keywords.
- ❏ Count the characters for the builder, i.e., USAJOBS: 5,000 characters; DoD*ESS/ AVUE: 4,000 characters for each work experience.
- ❏ Proofread and edit the resume – have a second person read the resume if you can.

Formatting for Resume Builders with the Outline Format

- ❏ Use ALL CAPS selectively with small paragraphs for your builder resume.
- ❏ The ALL CAPS keywords should match the keywords in the announcement.
- ❏ Paragraphs should be four to eight lines long.

Federal Resume Builders

- ❏ Copy and paste your resume into the various online builders.
- ❏ Preview the resume in the builder so you can correct any formatting problems.

DON'T!

- ❏ **Don't upload your resume. Use the resume builder instead.**

- ❏ Don't write one federal resume and use it for all of your positions.
- ❏ Don't just submit your TAP resume as your federal resume.
- ❏ Don't use too many acronyms.
- ❏ Don't copy and paste text straight from the announcement and your position description.
- ❏ Don't write your original resume in a builder (write the resume in software, then copy and paste into the builder).
- ❏ Don't write your federal resume in one paragraph (called the Big Block).
- ❏ Don't use a long list of bullets for your duties section.

- ❑ Use ALL CAPS for official position titles, titles of roles in jobs, or unofficial, working job titles, such as PROJECT MANAGER, SENIOR STAFF ADVISOR, RECEPTIONIST. All caps can be used to identify major functional areas of work. Do not overuse.

- ❑ Keep your paragraph length four to eight lines when possible—ten lines maximum.

- ❑ Use more nouns. Nouns are searchable terms in most databases. For example, use "editor" rather than "responsible for compiling documents and preparing a publication."

- ❑ Use plain language. Write professionally and concisely.

- ❑ Eliminate acronyms whenever possible. When you must use them, spell them out once.

- ❑ Space is limited, so drop words that do not add value.

- ❑ Avoid using the same descriptor twice in the same paragraph.

- ❑ Start each sentence with an action verb, and not "I." Use the personal pronoun "I" two times per page, to remind the reader that it is YOUR resume.

- ❑ Active voice is more powerful than passive voice.

- ❑ Use present tense for present work experience, past tense for previous work experience or for projects in the present work experience that have ended. Write in the first person, without the use of "I" and do not add "s" to your verbs, i.e., plans or manages.

- ❑ Include the proper names and generic descriptions of products, software, and equipment.

- ❑ Federal resumes must include compliance details for each job for the last ten years.

- ❑ Prior to ten years: if the positions are relevant, include the title of your job, organization, city, state, and dates. A short one-sentence description can be included.

- Begin with your most recent position and work backward, unless you need to highlight a position that is relevant and not the most recent.

- Military assignments: list the most recent ones first. Include many details on the last ten years. Anything prior to ten years ago, summarize and edit the text to include only the relevant experience.

- Retired Military: combine early positions/assignments.

- Students: include relevant positions only.

- Unpaid volunteer experience is equal to paid work experience for federal job qualifications. If you are using unpaid work to qualify, summarize your volunteer experience under Community Service and include the number of hours per week in your description.

- Missing years of experience? Just skip those years and write great descriptions about the positions you have held. However, be prepared to discuss it in an interview.

- Returning to government after leaving? Feature your GOVERNMENT EXPERIENCE first, then list your BUSINESS OR OTHER EXPERIENCE second.

Have You Heard That KSAs Have Been Eliminated?

The traditional essays for the Knowledge, Skills, and Abilities (KSAs) narratives were eliminated. President Obama signed a memorandum to make immediate hiring reforms on May 11, 2010. See details at www.opm.gov/hiringreform/.

Though you may no longer need to write long, cumbersome essays as part of your federal job application, you STILL need to somehow demonstrate that you do in fact have the knowledge, skills, and abilities to perform the job duties described in the vacancy announcement. How to do this will depend on the application.

Then How Will You Demonstrate Your KSAs?

KSAs are currently being covered in four sections of the federal application:

1. KSA Accomplishments in the Resume

2. KSA narratives to support the Questionnaire (on occasion 4,000 to 8,000 characters)

3. KSAs in the multiple choice Questionnaire

4. KSAs as part of the Behavior-Based Interview

The Outline Format can include your KSAs easily with the ALL CAP HEADINGS. You can feature COMMUNICATIONS, WRITING, PROJECT MANAGEMENT, PLANNING AND COORDINATING and other KSAs or significant competencies as headings. The text under the headings can be examples from your accomplishment record that will demonstrate your KSAs.

Definitions

Knowledge: An organized body of information, usually of a factual or procedural nature, which, if applied, makes adequate performance on the job possible.

Skills: The proficient manual, verbal, or mental manipulation of data, people, or things. Observable, quantifiable, measureable.

Abilities: The power to perform an activity at the present time. Implied is a lack of discernible barriers, either physical or mental, to performing the activity.

Write your KSA answers by giving examples that demonstrate that particular knowledge, skill, or ability.

KSAs Are Also Known As:

- Selective Placement Factors
- Narrative Statements
- Essays
- Examples
- Quality Ranking Factors
- Key Elements
- Specialized Qualifications
- Technical & Managerial Qualifications

How KSAs Are Still Included in Your Application

KSAs are now included in the federal resume to demonstrate that you have the knowledge, skills, and abilities to perform the position and therefore are not rated and ranked per se. However, KSAs are also covered in the Questionnaire with most applications. The Questionnaires are scored based on your answers. So the prior rating and ranking of KSAs are now gone, but KSAs are actually still part of the federal application within the resume and the Questionnaire.

★ TEN RULES FOR WRITING KSAS OR ACCOMPLISHMENTS

1 One excellent example per narrative will demonstrate that you have the knowledge, skills, and abilities for the position.

2 If possible and appropriate, use a different example in each accomplishment statement.

3 The typical length is 300 words or less.

WOW!

4 Write your accomplishment examples with specific details, including the challenge of the example and the results.

5 Spell out ALL acronyms.

6 Write in the first person. "I serve as a point-of-contact for all inquiries that come to our office."

7 Quantify your results and accomplishments.

8 Draw material from all parts of your life, including community service, volunteer projects, or training.

9 Limit your paragraphs to 6 to 8 lines long for readability.

10 Proofread your writing again and again.

Example #1: KSAs in the Resume

This example matches the federal resume to the required KSAs in the announcement.

Job Title: PUBLIC AFFAIRS SPECIALIST
Department: Department of the Army
Agency: U.S. Army Accession Command
Job Announcement Number: NEAJ12816501674933D

SPECIALIZED EXPERIENCE: Applicants must have one year of specialized experience at the GS-07 grade level to include the following areas: 1. Experience composing **written** documents such as newspaper articles/newsletters, news briefs, press releases, or feature articles for public media; 2. Experience utilizing current **social media networks** or video/digital formats to promote information, programs, events, or other newsworthy occurrences; and 3. Experience working with and **maintaining relationships** with individuals within and outside of an organization.

PARTNER/MANAGER   **09/2010 - 02/2012**

BaseCouponConnection.com, 47 Honeysuckle Lane, Fort Stewart, GA 31315
Salary: $2,160 per month, Hours per week: 70
Supervisor: Natalie Richards (Self), Phone: 912-463-3240, May contact.

(3) MARKETING PROGRAM FOR MILITARY FAMILIES WITH FAMILY MEMBER IN IRAQ. Developed, owned, managed and operated business that sold marketing contracts to local businesses. Marketed "Send It To Your Sweetie" program targeting free services to military families with members in Iraq for shipping, phone messages, and personal delivery of gifts for their loved ones. Met with base command to insure all regulations and policies were met.

- Accomplishment: Conceptualized a successful program for family members to send gifts and messages to military personnel. More than 2,500 messages were sent through this program in just six months. Sold business in less than 6 months for a substantial profit.

(1) COMMUNICATIONS. Wrote business plan and developed all aspects of advertising and marketing. Performed cold calls on business customers and followed up with written proposals. Created and delivered PowerPoint presentations to groups of various sizes. Organized and prepared mailings to families and businesses.

(2) WEBSITE DESIGN: Designed website and prepared spreadsheet to track monthly views and clicks. Due to volume of business, interviewed and hired 3 contractors to assist with billing, designing ads, and updating website.

EXAMPLE #2: Surprise Narrative KSAs in the Questionnaire

Sometimes after you complete the typical multiple-choice Questionnaire, you might be asked to write narratives to support your Questionnaire answers.

Questionnaire with Narrative Responses (4,000 characters)

Grade - 09 Questions

Based on your responses to the previous questions in this vacancy announcement, you've been forwarded to this additional phase. The following question(s) relate to the questions asked previously in this announcement. You can review your responses by using the Previous button. To successfully complete your application, please review and follow these instructions:

1. Respond to each question. If you do not have related experience, enter "N/A".

2. Your responses to all of the questions in this announcement must be substantiated by the information in your resume.

3. Select the "Next" button at the bottom of each screen to make sure that you have viewed and responded to all questions.

4. If you wish to save your responses and come back later to complete your application, enter placeholder text in any empty text fields, and click the "Next" button. For each web page, the system will time out after one hour of inactivity and your entries will be lost unless you select the "Next" button.

5. You can return to the vacancy and complete your application, but all information must be submitted by the closing date of the announcement.

6. Once you have responded to all questions, select the "Finish" button. The system requires that you select the "FINISH" button, or your application will not be saved; your application will be incomplete, and you will not be considered for this vacancy.

7. After selecting "FINISH" you will be returned to the USAJOBS site.

* 1. Describe your experience evaluating policies/implementing programs related to operation /maintenance of commercial buildings/leased space; analyzing the effectiveness/efficiency of building operations, equipment & automated systems; interacting with customers/stakeholders regarding building services to assess needs/recommend solutions; analyzing real property budgetary/financial data. Limit your response to 4,000 characters, which is approximately one typewritten page.
    Enter NA if Not Applicable.

4000 characters left (4000 character limit)

Vacancy Questions

Eligibility	Series Grade Location	Grade Specific Question	All Grade Questions	Documents	Application Review

All Grade Questions

Items marked with * are required.

All Grades Questions

Responses to the following questions will not be saved until you click the Next button. The system will time out after one hour unless you have clicked on the Next button to continue. It is recommended that you print the questions from the vacancy announcement and draft your responses before beginning the application process.

* 1. Do you have experience interacting directly with customers regarding building services and/or construction issues in order to assess customer needs and design solutions to meet those needs?

- ◉ Yes
- ◯ No

* 2. Please indicate which of the following best describes your experience maintaining and nurturing customer relationships to enhance customer loyalty and retention.

- ◯ I have not had experience performing this task.
- ◯ I have performed similar or directly related tasks and my experience or training has equipped me to perform these functions successfully.
- ◯ I have independently maintained and nurtured customer relationships to enhance customer loyalty and retention and only in unique or unusual situations did I require assistance or review by a supervisor or senior employee.
- ◯ I have assisted a senior staff member in maintaining and nurturing customer relationships to enhance customer loyalty and retention.
- ◉ I am highly skilled at maintaining and nurturing customer relationships to enhance customer loyalty and retention. I have performed this task routinely and have conducted training in this area.

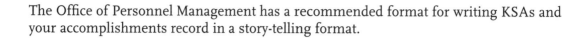

★ CCAR FORMAT

The Office of Personnel Management has a recommended format for writing KSAs and your accomplishments record in a story-telling format.

Introducing the Context, Challenge, Action, Result (CCAR) Model for writing better KSAs:

CONTEXT

The context should include the role you played in this example. Were you a team member, planner, organizer, facilitator, administrator, or coordinator? Also, include your job title at the time and the timeline of the project. You may want to note the name of the project or situation.

CHALLENGE

What was the specific problem that you faced that needed resolution? Describe the challenge of the situation. The problem could be disorganization in the office, new programs that needed to be implemented or supported, a change in management, a major project stalled, or a large conference or meeting being planned. The challenge can be difficult to write about. You can write the challenge last when you are drafting your KSAs.

ACTION

What did you do that made a difference? Did you change the way the office processed information, responded to customers, managed programs? What did you do?

RESULT

What difference did it make? Did this new action save dollars or time? Did it increase accountability and information? Did the team achieve its goals?

This CCAR story-telling format is also great for the Behavior-Based Interview. Write your accomplishment "stories" and prepare for the Interview Examination.

STEP 7

Please write a work or non-work related example to support a particular KSA or example required in an Assessment Questionnaire. Write your CCAR stories and accomplishments for the questionnaire examples, the Behavior-Based Interview, and a short version for your federal resume.

CONTEXT:

CHALLENGE:

ACTION:

1.

2.

3.

4.

RESULTS:

RECOGNITION/AWARD:

When KSAs are written on separate sheets of paper, the typical length is a 1/2 page for each, or 300 words or less. One or two examples can be written about to demonstrate your experience in this Knowledge, Skill, or Ability. These examples follow the CCAR story-telling formula.

It is still useful to write these KSA narratives for your Behavior-Based Interview to practice telling the story about your accomplishments.

---

1. **Knowledge of laws, rules, and regulations and ability to apply appropriate procedures in connection with payments, collections, or entitlements**

Context: In my Administrative Assistant position in the Finance Office, Rota, Spain for 14 months, I HANDLED PAY REQUESTS and problem-solving from both civilian and military personnel. Maintained knowledge of military pay and leave regulations as stated in the Code of Military Personnel Regulations.

Challenge: I was a point of contact for soldiers returning from specialized training and deployments throughout CONUS and OCONUS.

Actions: I researched and resolved complex pay issues for soldiers and officers in support of deployment activities, travel, and repayment of expenses. I investigated databases for payment information, and followed up to ensure they were paid.

Results: Communicated with Defense Finance and Accounting Office Vendor representatives in Indianapolis to research problems and ensure payment. Was successful at establishing a contact who was responsive to my inquiries within 24 to 48 hours for numerous problem payment requests.

2. Ability to reach sound and justifiable decisions and determine appropriate course of action, including the ability to extract and analyze information from a variety of sources.

Context: In Rota, Spain, I accepted an administrative office position with an outdated filing system and library of regulations. The files and regulations had not been organized or touched since the 1960s. The filing room was almost totally unusable with stacks of file folders, documents, and regulations approximately 8 feet tall.

Challenge: The files and library of regulations included more than 20 file cabinets and an entire wall of regulations. There were more than 250 notebooks of regulations and documents pertaining to personnel, readiness, payroll, and travel, which were significant when problem solving and researching complex cases of entitlement and pay issues.

Actions: I revamped and updated the unit's outdated filing system and library of regulations, bringing it in accordance with Navy regulations. I also developed an Excel spreadsheet which covered the regulations in the document room. This Excel file took one month to create with categories based on documents in the document library.

Results: This contributed to a 100 percent rating in a later Inspector General's (IG) inspection. Also, the reorganization of the files resulted in extensive time-savings for the CO and XO almost every day. Received recognition and cash award for this service contribution.

3. Ability to communicate orally.

Context: In my current position in Rota, Spain, I am the lead administrative assistant to the CO and XO for the U.S. Naval Base. I am experienced in representing the office with administrative information related to schedules, travel, and problem solving. I enjoy communicating with military personnel, family members, senior officers, and contractors.

An example of a particular experience where I demonstrated empathy and compassion in communications includes:

At Coronado NAS, I had the honor to be a volunteer administrative member of the first Warrior in Transition Program for the base.

Challenge: The major challenges were that this was the first organization of this type for Coronado and required interviewing and assessing the needs of the returning military from Iraq and Afghanistan and their family members.

Actions: I was trained to provide advocacy and services to family members to support special needs regarding health care services, critical medical services, and support for medical care. I communicated with military personnel and family members to refer services for medical care and assistance.

Results: The program is now established, and procedures and resources are set up for family members and military personnel who may be needing support from the Warrior in Transition Program. Coronado NAS has approximately 100 service members in the Warrior in Transition Program presently.

"...allow individuals to apply for Federal employment by submitting resumes and cover letters or completing simple, plain language applications, and assess applicants using valid, reliable tools..."

The White House, Office of the Press Secretary, May 11, 2010
Presidential Memorandum on Improving the Federal Recruitment and Hiring Process

Cover letters are now officially part of the federal application!

Specialized Experience

Add a list of skills and experience that you can offer that matches the Specialized Experience in the announcement.

Passion and Interest in the Mission

Write about your interest in the mission of the agency or organization. If you know the mission, can speak about it in a sentence, you can stand out above your competition.

Letter of Interest

The cover letter IS a letter of interest. You are interested in the job. The cover letter is more than a transmittal. Take this opportunity to sell your special qualifications, certification, training, and mission-related experiences. This is another small writing test.

Adding or Uploading a Short Cover Letter into the Resume Builder

With USAJOBS, you can add the letter into Additional Information section. With Application Manager, you can upload your cover letter.

Special Considerations

You can mention your willingness to relocate, eligibility for non-competitive spouse appointments, veterans' preference, reasons for wanting to move, such as family, and other special interest items in the cover letter.

Why Hire Me?

Be sure to mention your best qualities (that match the announcement).

Compelling?

Tell the reader why you are an excellent candidate and you believe in the mission of the agency.

Be sure to include announcement qualifications in your cover letter, such as: providing assistance to senior specialists in the evaluation and analysis of training programs; assisting in the execution of training programs by carrying out specified portions or segments of specific projects (e.g., preparing and coordinating training requests, advertising upcoming training, maintaining training attendance data, arranging training spaces and locations, identifying training needs and informing staff of upcoming training classes); and identifying and recommending solutions to training problems and providing advice to staff on established methods and procedures.

MELODY ANN RICHARDS
2222 Alexandria Boulevard
Falls Church, VA 22043
Phone: 703-333-3333
Email: _melody.richards@army.mil_

US Department of State
Application Evaluation Branch
2401 E Street, NW
Washington, DC 20522-0108
ATTN: John Jones
RE: MISSION SUPPORT SPECIALIST (TRAINING), Annct No: 30303

Dear Mr. Jones:

Enclosed are my application materials for the Mission Support Specialist (Training Coordinator) within the Foreign Service Institute, Department of State.

I can offer the Foreign Service Institute the following training and program coordination skills:

- Evaluating and analyzing training programs and curriculum
- Coordinating training programs by professional instructors
- Managing training space, training equipment needs
- Managing registrations and attendance
- Identifying and recommending training solutions to individuals and managers
- Recommending training techniques to improve evaluations and customer satisfaction

One of my strongest assets as a training administrator is my ability to manage complex international courses and programs and resolve problems related to instructors, curriculum, and technology.

I am dedicated to helping to coordinate international training programs for Department of State and other foreign affairs agencies to assist employees transitioning from full-time government work due to retirement or involuntary separation. I am highly detailed and can offer diplomacy and tact in communicating with State Department professionals and Foreign Service Officers.

I am willing to travel if needed and am planning to relocate to the DC area next month. I am available for an interview at your convenience.

Sincerely,
MELODY ANN RICHARDS

STEP 8

★ Apply for Jobs with USAJOBS

Currently, there are many ways to apply for federal jobs. If you have both a paper federal resume and an electronic resume prepared, you should be ready to apply to all of the jobs in their various required formats. After you apply to a few of the announcements, you will get faster and be able to adjust your resume to fit the application requirements.

Search Jobs Keyword Tips

What: (keywords)   Where: (city, state or zip code) ▶

Browse Jobs > | Advanced/International Search >

USAJOBS' Resume Builder allows you to create a uniform resume that provides all of the information required by government agencies. Instead of creating multiple resumes in different formats, you can build your resume once and be ready for all job opportunities.

Resume 1: Administrative / Analyst
View | Edit | Duplicate | Delete | Renew
Format: USAJOBS Resume
Source: Built with USAJOBS Resume Builder
Status: Searchable
Make Not Searchable
Expiration Date: 11/14/2011

Resume 2: Program and Management Analyst, GS-12
View | Edit | Duplicate | Delete
Format: USAJOBS Resume
Source: Built with USAJOBS Resume Builder
Status: Not Searchable
Make Searchable

Resume 3: Fedres Guidebook 4th Ed., before & after samples
View | Edit | Duplicate | Delete
Format: USAJOBS Resume
Source: Built with USAJOBS Resume Builder
Status: Not Searchable
Make Searchable

Resume 4: Noncompetitive Spouse Appt Federal Resume
View | Edit | Duplicate | Delete
Format: USAJOBS Resume
Source: Built with USAJOBS Resume Builder
Status: Not Searchable
Make Searchable

Build New Resume ▶   Upload New Resume ▶

You have created **4** of **5** possible resumes. You are able to upload and store **2** uploaded resumes; you have created **0** of **2** possible uploaded resumes.

Read the "how to apply" instructions, because they could be different for each announcement. Get ready to copy and paste into builders, answer questions, write short essays, and fax or upload your DD-214 and transcripts. Apply a day early if possible to navigate the automated application systems.

Be patient and consider each job and agency separately. Your perseverance will pay off. Learn how to copy and paste quickly. Use the control-A (select all), control-C (copy), and control-V (paste) commands. This will speed up your copy and paste submissions.

On left: screenshot of Kathryn Troutman's USAJOBS profile page.

Getting Started with USAJOBS

Use this getting started guide to set up your USAJOBS account and apply for federal jobs!

1. Logging In: Write Down Your Password!

Applicants routinely complain that they forget their password, which must include numbers, symbols, and letters. Make sure you link your account to a personal email, not a work email, so that you can access it at home.

2. Edit Your Profile: Answer Carefully!

The profile section of USAJOBS will pop up when you register or can be accessed by clicking on "Edit Profile" on the Main page.

You will be asked to enter Personal Information, Hiring Eligibility, Preferences, Demographic information, and Account Information.

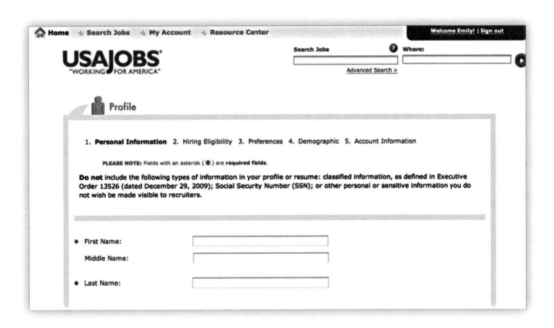

3. Personal Information

You can enter your career goal, but HR does not routinely read it. It could be more important if your resume is "searchable" and you have a unique skill set.

Current Goal

My Current Goal is:

Writer / Editor, GS 9/11

(476 characters remaining)

Highest Career Level Achieved: Mid–Career Professional

4. Eligibility

Your answers to these questions can determine whether or not your resume and application ever make it to human resources. So, answer carefully.

U.S. Citizen: Most federal jobs require citizenship.

Selective Service: If you are a man, did you sign up for the draft? Many times you may not remember doing so, but it is a normal part of getting a driver's license, voting, etc.

Contractors do not have "reinstatement eligibility."

Veterans' Preference: Veterans must know their preference eligibility.
See www.opm.gov/StaffingPortal/vetguide.asp#2Types

* 3. Are you a Veteran of the U.S. Armed Forces or are you eligible for "derived" preference? ● Yes ○ No

   3.1 Do you claim Veterans' Preference?

   ○ No, I do not claim Veterans' Preference

   ○ 5-point preference based on active duty in the U.S. Armed Forces (TP)

   ○ 10-point preference based on a compensable service connected disability of at least 10% but less than 30% (CP)

   ◉ 10-point preference based on a compensable service connected disability of 30% or more (CPS)

   ○ 10-point preference for non-compensable disability or Purple Heart (XP)

   ○ 10-point preference based on wife, widow, or widower preference (XP)

As veteran of the U.S. military, should I click "yes" in the "Applicant Eligibility" box even though I am not a current or former Federal employee?

Yes. In general, if you are preference eligible or have served at least 3 years of continuous active duty in the Armed Forces, you should click "yes" in the "Applicant Eligibility" box. You may apply for jobs that are open to U.S. citizens as well as jobs that are open to current and former Federal employees.

Many veterans miss the important point made above! Make sure you fill out questions 4 and 4.1 correctly if you are a veteran.

✽ 4. Please select the statement below which best reflects your Federal employment status (if applicable).

- ◯ I am not and have never been a Federal employee.
- ◉ I am currently a Federal employee.
- ◯ I am a former Federal employee with reinstatement eligibility.
- ◯ I am a former Federal employee but do not have reinstatement eligibility.

4.1 By which Federal agency and organization are you currently employed?

Select Department:

Department of Defense ▾

Select Agency:

Department of the Navy ▾

---

5. Eligibility Documentation

Veterans

When claiming preference, veterans must provide a copy of their DD-214, Certificate of Release or Discharge from Active Duty, or other acceptable documentation.

Applicants claiming 10-point preference will need to submit Form SF-15, Application for 10-point veterans' preference. Ensure your documentation reflects the character of discharge.

If you do not upload your documentation, you will not be eligible for veterans' preference.

Federal Employees

If you are a current federal employee, you must upload your SF-50, or you will not be considered for jobs open only to current feds.

6. Veterans Recruitment Appointment (VRA)

Veterans can choose their "VRA" hiring appointment eligibility.

Other questions include federal annuity, accepting a buyout, and ICTAP eligibility.

More information on VRA, RIF, ICTAP and federal "eligibility" status can be found here, "The Employee's Guide to Career Transition" from the Office of Personnel Management"–www.opm.gov/rif/employee_guides/career_transition.asp

---

4.2 Are you a current Federal employee serving under a Veterans' Recruitment Appointment (VRA)?
◯ Yes   ◯ No

4.3 Indicate the pay plan, series, grade level/pay band of the highest permanent graded position you ever held as a Federal Civilian Employee.

Pay Plan: [NO   ◆]

Occupational Series: [◆]

Highest Pay Grade: [   ]

4.4 Are you a retiree receiving a Federal annuity? ◯ Yes   ◯ No

4.5 Have you accepted a buyout from a Federal agency within the past 5 years? ◯ Yes   ⦿ No

4.6 Are you ICTAP Eligible? ◯ Yes   ⦿ No

---

7. Special Hiring Options

There are many government initiatives that give employment preference to specific and targeted segments of the population. The special hiring options include:

Veterans Recruitment Appointment (VRA): An excepted authority that allows agencies to appoint eligible veterans without competition if the veteran has received a campaign badge for service during a war or in a campaign or expedition; or is a disabled veteran; or has received an Armed Forces Service Medal for participation in a military operation; or is a recently separated veteran (within the last 3 years) and separated under honorable conditions. Appointments under this authority may be made at any grade level up to and including a GS-11 or equivalent. This is an excepted service appointment, which can be converted to competitive service after two years.

30% or More Disabled Veteran: A person who was separated under honorable conditions from active duty in the Armed Forces performed at any time and who has established the present existence of a service-connected disability rated at 30% or greater or is receiving compensation, disability retirement benefits, or pension because of a public statute administered by the Department of Veterans Affairs or a military department.

Disabled veterans who have completed a VA training program: A person who meets the definition of a disabled veteran and has successfully completed a program to receive training or work experience at VA.

Military Spouse: Military spouses are eligible under this authority if the active duty military spouse: 1) receives a Permanent Change of Station (PCS) move; 2) has a 100% disability rating; or 3) died while on active duty. Each of these categories has different eligibility criteria that must be met.

Certain Former Overseas Employees: A family member (which includes same-sex domestic partners) of a federal civilian employee or military member who has completed 52 weeks of service in a federal position overseas is eligible for appointment in the competitive service for a period of 3threeyears following the date of their return to the United States from the overseas area.

Schedule A Disabled Individuals with Intellectual Disabilities, Severe Physical Disabilities, or Psychiatric Disabilities may apply for non-competitive appointment through the Schedule A (5 C.F.R. 213.3102(u)) hiring authority. Documentation of the disability is required from a licensed medical professional; a licensed vocational rehabilitation specialist; or any federal, state, or District of Columbia agency or U.S. territory that issues or provides disability benefits.

VETERANS WHO ARE DISABLED SHOULD SELECT "SCHEDULE A DISABLED" IN ADDITION TO THEIR HIRING PREFERENCE IN QUESTION 4.

Special Hiring Options

Select from among the special hiring authorities listed below for which you are eligible.
(Please note that agencies will require documentation of eligibility prior to your appointment.)

Identification of eligibility for any special hiring authority is entirely voluntary, and you will not be subject to any adverse treatment if you decline to provide it. If you do not wish to volunteer this information at this time, you may still choose to apply for jobs, as they are announced, under any of these special hiring authorities for which you are eligible. If you volunteer to provide information here about the special hiring authorities for which you believe you are eligible, then agencies who are searching for potential applicants to hire under one of these authorities may be able to locate your resume through USAJOBS and invite you to apply. Otherwise, this information will be retained in the USAJOBS database and not disclosed. For information on each of the special hiring options below, please review the definitions on our Special Hiring Options page.

- ☑ Veterans Recruitment Appointment (VRA)
- ☑ 30% or More Disabled Veteran
- ☑ Disabled veterans who have completed a VA training program
- ☑ Military Spouse
- ☑ Certain former overseas employees
- ☑ Schedule A Disabled

---

8. Preferences

Applicants should choose carefully in this section because their answers will determine whether they are eligible later.

Are you willing to travel? If you say "No" you will be disqualified from a job, even if the amount of travel is very minimal.

What type of work are you willing to accept? Consider that more federal agencies are using "temp" and "term" jobs to fill positions when money is tight, or when the future is unknown. For example, many jobs that came out of the mortgage crisis were initially term jobs that eventually may become permanent.

If you accidentally apply for a "temp" or "term" job, but didn't click the button on this page, your application won't be read at all by human resources.

What type of work schedule are you willing to accept? Consider being flexible.

Select your desired work location(s). Select all of U.S. and if you apply for a job abroad, remember to come back and select that location as well.

If you only pick D.C., you might later be disqualified for a job in Baltimore.

9. Demographic

Your answers to this question are voluntary and do not affect whether or not you will be hired.

10. Personal Information

Write down your password! Also, you can choose to receive "Notification Alerts" on your application. This is important in case a job posting is pulled or re-announced.

Notification Settings

Notification Alerts enable you to stay informed of changes to your application status.

Select the items that you would like to be notified of via email. You may edit your preferences and unsubscribe at any time.

- ☑ When jobs I have applied to have closed.
- ☑ When jobs I have saved are scheduled to close in three days.
- ☑ When the status of an application I've submitted changes.

STEP 8

11. My Account Main Page

Edit Profile: Personal Information, Hiring Eligibility, Preferences, Demographic Information, and Account Information

Resumes: You can save up to five resumes in USAJOBS. That includes uploaded resumes and resumes built using the USAJOBS Resume Builder.

Saved Searches: Save your preferences for jobs you've searched in the past.

Saved Jobs: You can bookmark jobs you like.

Saved Documents: Your uploaded documents appear here. If you are using education to qualify for experience, you must upload your transcripts. They can be unofficial (HR will ask for official transcripts if you are hired).

Application Status: This section helps you track and follow up on your application and determine if you've actually applied.

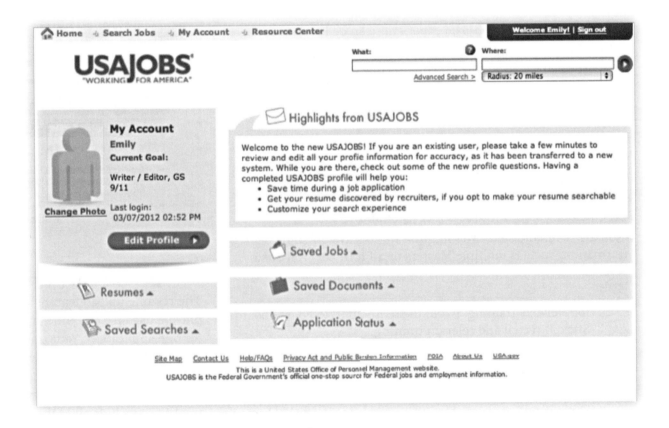

12. Resume Builder

Using the USAJOBS Resume Builder increases the chances that you will apply correctly for a federal job. Candidates who miss critical information on their resume will not be considered.

Work Experience

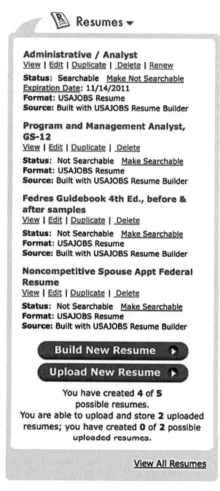

- ❏ No formatting or special characters like ampersand (&).
- ❏ Use ALL CAPS to highlight important words.
- ❏ Use small paragraphs to ensure readability.
- ❏ Jobs are listed strictly in chronological order.
- ❏ Drop jobs that are not recent or relevant. Human resources won't read past 15 years.
- ❏ Human Resources Specialists are looking for your "ONE YEAR SPECIALIZED EXPERIENCE." "One year" means 52 weeks, 40 hours per week. Locate this important section in each announcement.
- ❏ Ensure that all of your jobs and keywords are focused.
- ❏ Ensure human resources can qualify you by including salary.
- ❏ Education and non-paid experience can be listed as a job.
- ❏ If you are using education to qualify for your "one year specialized," you must include a copy of your transcripts.
- ❏ May we contact your supervisor? You may answer "no." It will not affect your application.

Education

Applicants for jobs with "positive education requirements", e.g., accountants, must list their courses and include credit hours.

Online degree programs must be accredited.

Don't include your GPA unless it is 3.5 or above.

If you are "overeducated," you might want to leave off some degree information, such as multiple Masters or a Ph.D. you don't use.

Other

- ❏ Job Related Training: Avoid the temptation to go overboard. Stick to recent and relevant training.

Additional Information:

- ❏ This section has 20,000 characters and could include anything.
- ❏ Some candidates use it for a "Professional Profile." Human resources probably won't read it, but the hiring official might.

References

Two references are not required, but they are recommended. Job-related references are best.

IMPORTANT TIP

The resume upload feature should only be used for one time and only for one application! Your uploaded resume might NOT get forwarded to the assessment questionnaire system. Also, the uploaded resume might not include all of the compliance details required by that agency. It is recommended to use the resume builder instead!

STEP 8

This automated system, run by USA Staffing, is frequently used in conjunction with USAJOBS, where https://applicationmanager.gov is the utility for administering the self-assessment and supplemental data questions. You will have the choice of pulling your resume from the USAJOBS online database, or you can upload your resume file. The upload allows greater flexibility in your resume presentation because you can format it however you like.

Step by Step: Application Manager with USAJOBS Resume Retrieval

1. Create a USAJOBS account and fill in your profile information.

2. Use the resume builder in "MY USAJOBS" to create your federal resume.

3. Find your announcement and click "APPLY ONLINE" to start the application process.

4. USAJOBS will ask you which version of your resume you want to use for that particular application. Select the one targeted for that job.

5. Your browser will then direct you to Application Manager to complete the biographical and eligibility information and start the Assessment Questionnaire.
   You will see that you must create a separate login for Application Manager.

6. Complete all questions and follow all steps including "UPLOAD DOCUMENTS."
   You will not upload a resume or KSA documents; however, you may need to upload or fax supplemental documents like transcripts or veterans' forms.

7. Follow all steps through "SUBMIT MY ANSWERS," or your application will not be submitted.

Step by Step: Application Manager with Resume Upload

1. Go to https://applicationmanager.gov and create your login and Profile.

2. Enter the job announcement number or USAJOBS control number (found in the USAJOBS vacancy announcement) to retrieve your target vacancy application.

3. Start the application and complete the biographical and eligibility information as well as the Assessment Questionnaire.

4. Upload and/or fax your resume and other pertinent application documents as well as other information that they might request—last evaluation, DD-214 (veterans), and transcripts, for example.

5. Follow all steps through "SUBMIT MY ANSWERS," or your application will not be submitted.

This commercial system is used by more than 30 agencies, including the U.S. Forest Service and U.S. Coast Guard. This application is a complex online form with questions and a profile. You submit your resume one time, and then apply for as many positions as you like in the database that Avue Central maintains. However, this can only be done for vacancies in agencies using this system.

Most jobs posted on AvueCentral.com are also posted on USAJOBS. That means that you can search for them in USAJOBS, where there is greater search flexibility and ease of use, and then apply to them through AvueCentral.com as instructed. You can go to AvueCentral. com directly; however, it is often easier to access the application by starting in USAJOBS and clicking "APPLY ONLINE."

Step by Step: AvueCentral

1. From the USAJOBS vacancy, click "APPLY ONLINE" and your browser will direct you to that particular vacancy in AvueCentral.com, or you can go directly to the Avue Central home page and search for the vacancy.

2. Log on or create your Profile in AvueCentral.com. Click "APPLY NOW" to start the application process.

3. On the left side of the screen, you will see a menu for filling in Mandatory information, such as your work history, education, and KSAs. The application will automatically pull your resume information from your Profile; however, you also have the option to revise it for the particular application.

4. Each vacancy announcement in Avue Central has "Job Posting Information" that includes the description that you saw posted in USAJOBS as well as the actual position description. Use this information to identify your keywords and write your resume content.

5. Once you have completed every section in Mandatory Information, you will click "SEND APPLICATION" to complete the process.

STEP 8

Agencies that are still using paper applications may allow several options for your application format. The package usually contains the following: cover letter, federal resume, KSAs, and supplemental information (such as transcripts).

The package is typically mailed, faxed, or hand delivered. You may use the U.S. Postal Service or other delivery method to transport your package.

We recommend that you use the preferred paper format, a federal resume. Also in the announcement, usually at the end, is the address to which to send your materials, a number to which to fax it, and perhaps instructions on how to apply with email. If you mail your application, get a delivery confirmation receipt. If you are facing a deadline, fax or email will deliver your application the same day. Whatever the method, if you send your materials ahead of the deadline, you will have time to phone the office to confirm receipt.

Your paper application should include the following:

- ❏ A nicely formatted federal resume printed on good quality paper
- ❏ KSA narratives (a separate document)
- ❏ A cover letter (if allowed)
- ❏ Required supplemental information such as photocopies of transcripts

A human resources specialist will receive your envelope, review the resume for basic qualifications and status, and then rate and rank your KSAs manually by reading for keywords and content. The top candidates will be referred to the hiring supervisor.

Step by Step: Non-Automated Applications

1. Focus your federal resume (with formatting) on the announcement, picking up the keywords and top skills from the duties, qualifications, and evaluation sections.

2. Add the job title, grade, series, and announcement number to the top of the resume and KSAs. Also, always include your name and the last four digits of your Social Security Number.

3. Write your KSAs for the position. Some applications provide a questionnaire for you to answer, print out, and submit.

4. Mail, fax, or email your application to the address (follow their directions). Never use a government postage-paid envelope. If faxing, follow cover sheet instructions exactly.

5. Send other information that they may request such as last performance evaluation (if you have one—not mandatory), transcripts, and DD-214. Do not send any attachments if they do not ask for any.

STEP 9

★ **Track and Follow Up on Your Applications**

Learn how to follow up and manage your federal job search campaign. Since the automated systems are so popular with federal agencies now, many of them include an automated reply system, as well as an online page where you can check the status of your applications. Some people can even read the notice, "you have been offered the position" online.

A federal job applicant can follow-up by phone on some job announcements as well. Those that include a name and phone number make follow up possible. It's important to keep track of your applications. Keep the announcements, and follow up on those that include a name and phone number after four to six weeks.

How Long Does It Take to Fill Federal Job?

The current goal for length of time to fill a federal vacancy is 45 days from the date of posting job announcement. However, in our experience, the curent average time seems to be more around the range of 90 to 120 days.

How People Are Hired: The Competitive Process

Identify Job and Assessments

Recruit and Announce Job

Accept and Review Applications

Assess Applicants

Certify Eligibles

Select

USAJOBS & Application Manager

Most of the automated application systems have tracking systems where you can check the status of your application. Be sure to check your status regularly. Save your user name and password for each builder.

Find Out Your Application Score Online

You can check on the status of your applications in both USAJOBS and Application Manager. Look for the Notification of Results (NOR), which will tell you the outcome of your application.

Emails from Human Resources

The May 11, 2010 Presidential Memorandum issued by the White House on *Improving the Federal Recruitment and Hiring Process* recommends the use of emails by HR specialists to inform applicants about the status of their application and the vacancy announcement. If you receive an email from the HR specialist concerning your qualifications for the position and you can't understand the email, just write back or call to get clarification of the email.

Sample Telephone Message Script

"Hello, I'm Kathryn Troutman. I'm calling regarding my application submitted for announcement number 10505 for Writer-Editor, GS-12. The closing date was 3/31 and I'm checking on the status of the recruitment. I can be reached at 410-744-4324 from 9 until 5, Monday through Friday, Eastern Standard Time. If you get voicemail, you can leave a message regarding the position. Thank you for your time. I look forward to your information."

Emailing the HR Representative

If there is an email address on the announcement, you could try contacting the human resources specialist by email. You can contact the HR specialist to check on the status of your applications and find out what your application score if this information is not posted online. Here is a sample letter:

> Subject line: Status of announcement 10101
>
> Dear Ms. Jones,
>
> I submitted my Federal resume, KSAs, and evaluation for the position of Writer-Editor, announcement no. 10101 on Dec. 22 by USPS. I'd like to check the status of my application and the recruitment, please.
>
> Is it still open and was I found qualified? Thank you very much for your time.
>
> Sincerely,
>
> Kathryn Troutman, SSN: 000-00-0000
>
> Daytime phone: 410-744-4324 (M-F EST) messages okay

★ CATEGORY RATING

What Happens to Your Application?

Category Rating is the ranking and selection process that is now mandatory under Presidential Memorandum, May 11, 2010. We are currently in a time of transition between the previous point system (rate and rank) and the new category rating system.

No More Scores

Under category rating, there is no disclosure of crediting plans (points) and/or rating schedules with scoring keys.

Three Buckets of Applicants

All of the applications are evaluated and sorted into three groups, which we like to call buckets.

- Best Qualified – This is the <u>only</u> group that will get Referred to the Supervisor.

- Well-Qualified – This group will <u>not</u> be referred.

- Qualified – This group will <u>not</u> be referred.

Minimum Requirements

All applicants who meet the basic qualification requirements established for the position are ranked by being assigned to the appropriate quality category based upon the job-related assessment tool(s) – the questionnaire!

"If you're not in the top bucket,
you're not in the game!"

– Kathryn Troutman

STEP 9

The following steps demonstrate how veterans' preference is applied in category rating.

1. Applicants are rated.

Their applications are evaluated and they are given one of three ratings, such as Good, Better, and Best.

2. Additional points are assigned based on type of veterans' preference.

- CPS: disability of 30% or more (10 points)
- CP: disability of at least 10% but less than 30% (10 points)
- TP: served at specific time and not disabled (5 points)
- XP: less than 10% disability or derived preference for certain family members (10 points)

3. CPS and CP rise to the top of the highest quality category.

Qualified preference eligibles with a compensable service-connected disability of 30% or more (CPS) and those with a compensable service-connected disability of more than 10% but less than 30% (CP) are placed at the top of the highest quality category.

	Status	Rating	Preference	Bucket
Dom	Disabled vet	Good	CP	Best Qualified
Chris	Non-disabled vet	Best	TP	Best Qualified
Anne	Non-vet	Best		Best Qualified
Mario	Non-vet	Best		Best Qualified
Sheila	Non-disabled vet	Better	TP	Well Qualified
Betty	Non-vet	Better		Well Qualified
Cory	Non-disabled vet	Good	TP	Qualified
Suzie	Non-vet	Good		Qualified
Aida	Non-vet	Good		Qualified

This sample pool of applicants demonstrates how the CP applicant rose to the top of the group even though the rating for that particular applicant was good and not best.

🗸 Application Status

IMPORTANT! If you did not apply to the job announcement with your USAJOBS resume through the apply online button, we cannot track your application. It is not possible to track applications in your USAJOBS account when they have been submitted through an agency's application website or through the mail. You can contact the agency that posted the announcement to verify receipt of your application. Each record will be deleted 18 months after Initial Application Date. You may want to print this page for future reference.

Applications 1 to 20   Page: [1] **[2] [3] [4] [5] [6] [7] [8] [9]**   Page 1 of 9

Initial Application Date ▼	Job Summary	Job Status	Agency Name	Last Application Update	Application Status	USAJOBS Uploaded Document Status
5/17/2010	**Resolutions & Receiverships Spec (WIP-PCAM), CG-1101-13** Job Announcement Number: 2010-TSO-ATL-0332 Pay Plan: CG-1101-13/13 Location: US-FL-Jacksonville	Active	Federal Deposit Insurance Corporation	5/17/2010	Application Status not Available	None more information...
5/17/2010	**Realty Specialist** Job Announcement Number: ADS10-R4-DNF-03407DP (PH) Pay Plan: GS-1170-11/09 Location: US-UT-Panguitch	Closed	Forest Service	5/17/2010	Application Status not Available	None more information...
5/17/2010	**MANAGEMENT AND PROGRAM ANALYST** Job Announcement Number: CIS-PJN-344956-ICS Pay Plan: GS-0343-13/12 Location: US-DC-WASHINGTON	Closed	Citizenship and Immigration Services	5/17/2010	Application Incomplete more information...	None more information...
5/14/2010	**Veterans Service Representative** Job Announcement Number: VB347790--MB Pay Plan: GS-0996/07 Location: US-CO-Lakewood	Closed	Veterans Benefits Administration	5/14/2010	Application Status not Available	None more information...
5/14/2010	**Health Insurance Specialist** Job Announcement Number: HHS-CM-CSQ-2010-0045 Pay Plan: GS-0107-13/13 Location: US-MD-Baltimore (Woodlawn)	Closed	Centers for Medicare & Medicaid Services	5/14/2010	Application Status not Available	None more information...
5/14/2010	**Administrative Tech (OA)** Job Announcement Number: NCAN10929543D Pay Plan: YB-0303-01/01 Location: US-DC-DC - Washington	Closed	Army Medical Command	5/14/2010	Application Status not Available	None more information...
5/14/2010	**Administrative Tech (OA)** Job Announcement Number: NCAN10929543D Pay Plan: YB-0303-01/01 Location: US-DC-DC - Washington	Closed	Army Medical Command	5/14/2010	Application Status not Available	None more information...

Application Manager

Main · Important Links · Help · Logout

user: **ktroutman**

My Application Packages
(Click a row to see a checklist of all the items you need to complete your application package, and the status of each.)

Vacancy ID : 145961 — Job Title : SPECIAL ASSISTANT

Status	Modified Date	Closing Date	USAJOBS Control Number
Complete	7/19/2007 8:31:03 AM	07/19/2007	949266

Vacancy ID : 256569 — Job Title : Human Resources Specialist

Status	Modified Date	Closing Date	USAJOBS Control Number
Closed - Not Submitted	4/30/2010 12:21:42 PM	04/30/2010	1547584

Vacancy ID : 286679 — Job Title : Mission Support Specialist

Status	Modified Date	Closing Date	USAJOBS Control Number
NOT SUBMITTED	5/3/2010 10:52:13 PM	09/21/2010	1683360

Vacancy ID : 308266 — Job Title : Physical Scientist DR-1301-2/3/4

Status	Modified Date	Closing Date	USAJOBS Control Number
Closed - Not Submitted	3/31/2010 5:31:51 PM	03/31/2010	1765405

Vacancy ID : 314268 — Job Title : INFORMATION TECHNOLOGY SPECIALIST (INFO SEC)

Status	Modified Date	Closing Date	USAJOBS Control Number
NOT SUBMITTED	3/22/2010 8:38:11 PM	06/19/2010	1788232

Vacancy ID : 314477 — Job Title : Program Analyst (Section 508), GS-0343-12/13

Status	Modified Date	Closing Date	USAJOBS Control Number
Closed - Not Submitted	4/7/2010 11:04:00 AM	04/07/2010	1825031

Vacancy ID : 318355 — Job Title : Management & Program Analyst

Status	Modified Date	Closing Date	USAJOBS Control Number
NOT SUBMITTED	2/22/2010 3:07:49 PM	08/11/2010	1803306

Vacancy ID : 328400 — Job Title : Security Specialist, GS-0080-11/12

Status	Modified Date	Closing Date	USAJOBS Control Number
Closed - Not Submitted	4/14/2010 3:37:00 PM	04/16/2010	1840057

Vacancy ID : 332071 — Job Title : Paralegal Specialist

Status	Modified Date	Closing Date	USAJOBS Control Number
Closed - Not Submitted	4/17/2010 4:42:11 PM	04/26/2010	1851491

Vacancy ID : 332930 — Job Title : PROCUREMENT ANALYST

Status	Modified Date	Closing Date	USAJOBS Control Number
Closed - Not Submitted	4/26/2010 10:39:13 PM	04/26/2010	1871607

Vacancy ID : 333252 — Job Title : Staff Assistant

Status	Modified Date	Closing Date	USAJOBS Control Number
Closed - Not Submitted	3/29/2010 3:19:00 PM	03/29/2010	1856004

Vacancy ID : 333427 — Job Title : PROGRAM ANALYST (STRATEGIC PLANNER)

Status	Modified Date	Closing Date	USAJOBS Control Number
Closed - Not Submitted	4/30/2010 8:53:49 AM	05/06/2010	1865989

Vacancy ID : 333539 — Job Title : Administrative Officer

Status	Modified Date	Closing Date	USAJOBS Control Number
Closed - Not Submitted	5/6/2010 9:27:40 PM	05/07/2010	1883743

Notice of Results (NOR) gives you information about the status of your application. The types of responses could be: Not Eligible, Eligible, Best Qualified, Best Qualified and Not Among the Most Qualified to be Referred, Best Qualified and Referred. It's important to check your NORs, so that you can gauge the success of your applications.

You can find your Notice of Results in Applicationmanager.gov under My Application Packages. Click on the link to open up the announcement and results page. There you will find your messages, including your NORs.

Messages

	Message Type	Date Emailed	Date Printed
View	Cancellation Letter		7/26/2011 12:49:10 PM
View	Notification Letter		6/2/2011 2:25:40 PM

Here are some examples of the types of results you will see when you check your NORs.

Dear KATHRYN K TROUTMAN,

This refers to the application you recently submitted to this office for the position below:

Vacancy ID:	446111
Position:	Human Resources Specialist (Employee Benefits), GS-201-12
Announcement:	11D-123-YS
Agency:	OHCM HumanCapitalManagementDC

Spec Code:	003
Spec Title:	US Citizens
Grade:	12
Rating:	IE

Referral Name: AP-11-YRS-02020S0

Status: IN - Ineligible

Vet Pref:

Locations:

Washington DC Metro Area, DC

Status Code	Status Message
IN - Ineligible	We have carefully reviewed your application and determined that you are not eligible for the position with this Status code. Please refer to the rating codes and message description.

Rating Code	Rating Message
IE	Your application does not show that you have the length of specialized/specific experience needed for this specialty and grade.

Spec Code:	Spec Title:		Grade:	Rating:
002	Noncompetitive Merit Promotion		15	IAOC

Rating Code:	Rating Message:
IAOC	You are outside the area of consideration.

NOTICE OF RESULTS

Announcement Number 1203039KSDE
Occupation Construction Control Representative
Series/Grade GS-0809G-07
Location Norfolk, VA
Rating 98.61
Veterans Preference NOT A VET
Eligible/Ineligible Not Evaluated

This notice is a record of your application for Federal employment for the vacancy shown above. Under the Office of Personnel Management's regulations for considering applications under Delegated Examining, eligible applicants are considered based on the rating they receive and veteran's preference entitlements.

Your rating (score) shown above is based solely on your answers to the vacancy questions. Because your rating was not within the range for referral for this vacancy, your application was not evaluated for qualifications and your name was not referred to the selecting official for further consideration.

Spec Code:	Spec Title:	Grade:	Rating:
002	Human Resources	04	96
002	Human Resources	05	96
002	Human Resources	06	96
002	Human Resources	07	ID

Rating Code: Rating Message:
ID   You do not meet the minimum education and/or experience requirements for this specialty and grade.

For this vacancy, we referred the names of preference eligible veterans in the top category. Therefore, your name will not be referred to the selecting official at this time. If we receive a request from the program for additional candidates, your application may be reviewed for possible referral.

STEP 10

★ Interview for a Federal Job

Your first goal for the interview is to stand out above the competition with your relevant skills, experiences, and your ability to communicate them to the hiring manager. Second, you want to impress the hiring team that YOU CAN DO THE JOB being offered. And third, you need to demonstrate confidence, interest, and enthusiasm. This combination of solid relevant content and examples, efficient communications skills, and confident delivery method does not come naturally to most people.

It takes practice, research, and preparation for a successful job interview.

You will see typical questions that could be asked in an interview. Most panel members or individual supervisor/interviewers will prepare seven to ten questions. The same questions are asked of all the interviewees. The answers are graded. So, be prepared to give examples that demonstrate your knowledge, skills, and abilities.

If you have written your KSAs from Step 7, the KSA narrative/examples could be the basis of your accomplishments for the Behavior-Based Interview. But you will have to practice speaking about your accomplishments. Even the most seasoned speakers, briefers, and media experts take training in speaking, presentation, and content development. Jobseekers should spend more time writing examples (their "message") that support their best strengths, and practice speaking these elements. A great interview can get you hired. But interviewing is not easy for anyone.

Be prepared for a new interview format, the Behavior-Based Interview. Be prepared to give examples in answers to seven to ten questions that will be situation or experience based. If you have an example of how you led a team, provided training, or managed a project, be prepared to talk about the project and teamwork. The best answers will be examples that demonstrate your past performance.

Know the paperwork

Know the vacancy announcement, agency mission, and office function. Read your resume and KSAs out loud with enthusiasm. Become convinced that you are very well qualified for the job and that the agency NEEDS you to help achieve their mission.

Do the necessary research

Go online to research the agency, department, and position. Read press releases about the organization. Go to www.washingtonpost.com and search for the organization to see if there are any recent news events.

Practice

In front of a mirror, tape recorder, video camera, family member, friend, anyone who volunteers to listen to you.

Confidence, Knowledge, and Skills

In order to "sell" yourself for a new position, you have to believe in your abilities. Read books and listen to tapes that will help boost your confidence and give you the support you need to "brag" on your work skills. Don't forget or be afraid to use "I"!

Telephone Interview

Prepare as though you are meeting the person in an office. Get dressed nicely, have your papers neatly organized, create a quiet environment, and project a focused listening and communications style. If you are great on the phone, you can get a second interview.

Individual

For the one-on-one interview, get ready for an unknown Q&A format. Prepare your questions and answers ahead of time and be ready. Be friendly, professional, and answer the questions. Practice for this interview.

Group/Panel Interview

Two to six professional staff will interview and observe your answers. This is a difficult interview format, but it is not used too often. Just look at the person asking the question while he or she is speaking. Answer the question by looking at the person asking, but look around the room as well.

Tell Me About Yourself

Write a three-minute introduction that you could use in an interview. It should include information relevant to the position.

A Significant Accomplishment

Write one significant accomplishment that you will describe in an interview:

Select Your Best Competencies

Make a list of your best core competencies:

Write Your Most Critical Skills

Make a list of your best skills that will be most marketable to this employer:

Typical interview questions will be:

J	Job Related
O	Open Ended
B	Behavior-Based
S	Skill and Competency Based

Competency-Based Sample Interview Questions

Often, an interviewer will ask questions that directly relate to a competency required for the position. Here are some examples.

- **Attention to Detail:** Describe a project you were working on that required attention to detail.

- **Communication:** Describe a time when you had to communicate under difficult circumstances.

- **Conflict Management:** Describe a situation where you found yourself working with someone who didn't like you. How did you handle it?

- **Continuous Learning:** Describe a time when you recognized a problem as an opportunity.

- **Customer Service:** Describe a situation in which you demonstrated an effective customer service skill.

- **Decisiveness:** Tell me about a time when you had to stand up for a decision you made even though it made you unpopular.

- **Leadership:** Describe a time when you exhibited participatory management.

- **Planning, Organizing, Goal Setting:** Describe a time when you had to complete multiple tasks. What method did you use to manage your time?

- **Presentation:** Tell me about a time when you developed a lesson, training, or briefing and presented it to a group.

- **Problem Solving:** Describe a time when you analyzed data to determine multiple solutions to a problem. What steps did you take?

- **Resource Management:** Describe a situation when you capitalized on an employee's skill.

- **Team Work:** Describe a time when you had to deal with a team member that was not pulling his/her weight.

Present your best competencies with a great story or example that demonstrates your real behavior.

LEADERSHIP – Inspires, motivates, and guides others toward strategic/operation goals and corporate values. Coaches, mentors, and challenges staff and adapts leadership style to various situations. Consistently demonstrates decisiveness in day-to-day actions. Takes unpopular positions when necessary. Faces adversity head on. Rallies support and strives for consensus to accomplish tasks. Leads by personal example. Demonstrates concern for employees' welfare and safety, by continuously monitoring and eliminating potentially hazardous or unhealthy work situations.

Can you give me an example where you lead a team?

CONTEXT:

CHALLENGE:

ACTION:

     1.

     2.

     3.

RESULTS:

Kathryn K. Troutman,
Author and President
The Resume Place, Inc.

Photo by Emily Troutman

1. Founder, President, and Manager of The Resume Place®, the first federal job search consulting and federal resume writing service in the world, and the producer of www.resume-place.com, the first website devoted to federal resume writing.

2. Pioneer designer of the federal resume format in 1995 with the publication of the leading resource for federal human resources and jobseekers worldwide—the *Federal Resume Guidebook*.

3. Developer of the Ten Steps to a Federal Job®, a licensed curriculum and turnkey training program taught by more than 1,000 Certified Federal Job Search Trainers™ (CFJST) around the world.

4. Leading Federal Resume Writing, KSA, Resumix, ECQ and Federal Interview government contracted trainer. GSA Schedule Holder.

5. Author of numerous federal career publications (in addition to the *Federal Resume Guidebook* mentioned above):

The *Military to Federal Career Guide* is the first book for military personnel and is now in its 2nd edition, featuring veteran federal resumes. Troutman recognized the need for returning military personnel from Iraq, Afghanistan, and Kosovo to have a resource available to them in their searches for government jobs.

Ten Steps to a Federal Job was published two months after 9/11 and was written for private industry jobseekers seeking first-time positions in the federal government, where they could contribute to our nation's security. Now in its 3rd edition.

The *Jobseeker's Guide* started initially as the companion course handout to the *Ten Steps* book, but captured its own following when it became the handout text used by over 200 military installations throughout the world for transitioning military and family members. Now in its 5th edition.

With the looming human capital crisis and baby boomers retiring in government, the *Student's Federal Career Guide* was co-authored with Kathryn's daughter and MPP graduate, Emily Troutman, and is the first book for students pursuing a federal job. Now in its 2nd edition, including the latest information on the changing structure of student programs, plus additional guidance for veterans taking advantage of the Post-9/11 GI Bill.

Resumes for Dummies (5th edition) by Joyce Lain Kennedy is currently in its 5th edition and is renowned as the premier guidebook for resume writing. Kathryn and The Resume Place staff served as designers and producers of all the private industry resume samples.

Ironically enough, Paulina Chen came from the federal government to work with Kathryn Troutman and The Resume Place®.

Paulina was working at the U.S. Environmental Protection Agency developing printed materials when Kathryn came to the EPA to provide federal resume consultations. Kathryn noticed Paulina's ability to communicate complex information in a straightforward, easy-to-understand way. When Paulina expressed her desire to eventually become a freelance graphic designer, Kathryn offered Paulina her first freelance opportunity—to design and lay out the interior pages for the first edition of *Ten Steps to a Federal Job*.

Paulina Chen

Photo by Emily Troutman

Now many years later, this team is still collaborating, and the *Jobseeker's Guide 5th Edition* is their book project together. Paulina also assists The Resume Place and the Federal Career Training Institute with their websites and marketing efforts.

Paulina's degree in Product Design from Stanford University gave her the solid technical and aesthetic fundamentals that she applies to her print and web design. She was also certified by the USDA Graduate School in desktop publishing.

Paulina has helped The Resume Place and other clients with writing and designing books, catalogs, logos, business cards, promotional materials, and websites. She can be reached at paulinachen@livingwaterdesigns.com.

★ VETERAN FEDERAL CAREER CONSULTING AND RESUME WRITING SERVICES

We have trained writers who specialize in translating military experience into skills and qualifications for federal positions. We can help you with an outstanding federal resume that can get you referred to a supervisor.

We are pleased to offer America's veterans the following:

- We regularly offer a special 5% discount on veteran career consultation, full service federal resumes, and cover letters.

The Resume Place Resume writers and editors will:

- Review resumes drafted by the veteran
- Determine or confirm best occupational series and grade for the veteran
- Ensure that One Year Specialized Experience is evident for the target positions
- Edit and feature improved keywords for an announcement or classification standard
- Review or confirm accomplishments
- Review and improve format and content
- Finalize the resume in Outline Format with keywords and accomplishments

Get help applying for federal jobs with USAJOBS 3.0:

- USAJOBS 3.0 account and builder setup.
- Document uploads, including veterans' documents, transcripts, cover letter, evaluations.
- Questionnaire review and completion.
- Submission and tracking & follow-up lessons.
- Announcement review for next announcements and job search strategies.

Check out these useful websites:

- *Free Federal Resume Builder, KSA Builder, Cover Letter Builder and Application Writing Builders* www.resume-place.com/resources/free-builders/

- *VetFedJobs* http://vetfedjobs.org/

- *Feds Hire Vets* www.fedshirevets.gov/

- *Mil2FedJobs (State of Maryland)* www.dllr.state.md.us/mil2fedjobs/

The Resume Place, Inc.
www.resume-place.com
888-480-8265
Federal Resume Writing since 1996
Authors of the first book on Federal Resume Writing:
the *Federal Resume Guidebook*

PUBLICATIONS BY THE RESUME PLACE®

  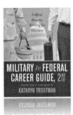    

Order online at www.resume-place.com | Career Center Orders: (410) 744 4324 or (888) 480 8265
FREE SHIPPING to centers and bases in the domestic US and APO; shipping is calculated for HI and overseas

Jobseeker's Guide, 5th Edition
Military to Federal Career Transition Resource Workbook and guide for the Ten Steps to a Federal Job® training curriculum. Federal job search strategies for first-time jobseekers who are separating military and family members. *$14.95 ea., Bulk Rates Available*

Ten Steps to a Federal Job & CD-ROM, 3rd Ed.
Written for a first-time applicant, particularly those making a career change from private industry to federal government. Case studies include 24 before & after samples of successful resumes! *$14.95 ea., Bulk Rates Available*

Federal Resume Guidebook & CD-ROM, 5th Ed.
The ultimate guide in federal resume, KSA, and ECQ writing. 30+ samples on the CD-ROM. Easy to use as a template for writing. Specialty occupational series chapters. *$31.95 ea., Bulk Rates Available*

Military to Federal Career Guide & CD-ROM, 2nd Ed.
Federal Resume Writing for Veterans
All samples and insight for military to federal transition for veterans. Samples are in the Outline Format with keywords, accomplishments from military careers. CD-ROM includes all samples and KSAs for military transition. *$14.95 ea., Bulk Rates Available*

Student's Federal Career Guide, 2nd Ed.
Winner, Best Careers Book of the Year, 2004. Outstanding book for jobseekers who are just getting out of college and whose education will help the applicant get qualified for a position. 20 samples of recent graduate resumes with emphasis on college degrees, courses, major papers, internships, and relevant work experiences. Outstanding usability of samples on the CD-ROM. *$14.95 ea., Bulk Rates Available*

Creating Your High School Resume & CD-ROM, 3rd Ed., and Instructor's Guide
Used in high school, military teen career programs, school-to-work programs worldwide. Samples of high school resumes—including those targeting ROTC, College, Certification Programs, Jobs, Military Scholarship/ Schools. Instructor's CD and Guide with PPTs and exercises. *$16.95 ea.*

Online Federal Resume Database
This Online Federal Resume Database contains more than 110 resume samples and federal job search resources from the current Resume Place publications. Each CD-ROM has a clearly organized interface. Sample resumes are available in Word and PDF format for quick previewing and easy editing. *Individual and Agency / Base Licenses Available*

★ CERTIFIED FEDERAL JOB SEARCH TRAINER™ (CFJST) AND
FEDERAL CAREER COACH® (CFCC) PROGRAM

A few of our 2012 classes

Since 1992, over 1000 other career professionals have benefitted from our unique certification in the Ten Steps to a Federal Job® curriculum, and the program continues to grow each year. Get certified and licensed to teach Kathryn Troutman's popular, proven, turnkey curriculum: Ten Steps to a Federal Job® and Federal Resume & KSA Writing curriculum. This course was developed by Kathryn Troutman as a direct result of her training experiences for hundreds of federal agencies throughout the world.

Our three day program is pre-approved to fulfill 24 continuing education hours for the Center of Credentialing and Education's Global Career Development Facilitator (GCDF) certification.

Registration Benefits - Incredible Value!

- Free Multi-User License to Our Ten Steps Online Resources (three months)
- Online Federal Resume Database
- Ten Steps eLearning Program
- Federal Career Books for Your Library:
  ◊ *Federal Resume Guidebook, 5th Edition*
  ◊ *The New SES Application*
  ◊ *Jobseeker's Guide, 5th Edition*
  ◊ *Ten Steps to a Federal Job* & CD-ROM, 3rd Edition
  ◊ *Military to Federal Career Guide* & CD-ROM, 2nd Edition
  ◊ *The Student's Federal Career Guide* & CD-ROM
  ◊ *Creating Your High School Resume* & CD-ROM
  ◊ Beautiful Ten Steps bag
- PowerPoint Presentations:
  ◊ Ten Steps to a Federal Job® – Licensed for two years
  ◊ Federal Hiring Program
  ◊ Veteran's and Spouse Hiring Programs
  ◊ Student Federal Hiring Programs

"I just wanted to let you know that attendance at the 3 - day course in March [2012] has done wonders for my confidence and wonders for my clients. When we go through the OPM Job Factors and the Grading of GS positions, most clients are over-joyed to have opened the "treasure chest" where the mystery of pursuing a Federal Job Position is solved. Thank you for all that you do!! I love the books and find something new EVERY day that I can share with my fellow coaches."

More Information and Registration
www.fedjobtraining.com/certification-programs.htm